REDEMPTIVE JUSTICE

FOR THE FALSELY ACCUSED, YOU'VE ALREADY WON

THOR STONE

First Paperback edition March, 2023

Manufactured in the United States of America

Scriptures referred to in this book are taken from the most up to date translations of the Holy Bible published by Zondervan Publishing House and provided online by biblegateway.com.

The stories in this book reflect the author's recollection of events. Some names, locations, and identifying characteristics have been changed to protect the privacy of those depicted. Dialogue has been re-created from memory.

Published by Victory Vision Publishing and Consulting
www.victoryvision.org

Imprint: Thor's Stone, LLC

Paperback ISBN: 979-8-9874498-0-6
eBook ISBN: 979-8-9874498-1-3

DEDICATION

This book is dedicated to all the men out there that have been falsely accused of sexual misconduct. You are not alone. May the Lord bless you and keep you and make His face shine upon you.

May you experience supernatural favor from the Lord. May your testimony be an inspiration about the goodness of God. And may the rest of your days be incredible!

CONTENTS

ACKNOWLEDGMENTS

I would first like to thank Joe and Betty. Your encouragement to write this book, which completely took me by surprise, was the first domino. When I resigned from my job and relocated to another state, I was determined to never speak of what happened to me, like it never happened. A fresh start elsewhere is what I needed and desired, so writing a book about the nightmare I had just left in my rear-view mirror, never entered my mind. Nobody needed to know. And then, after a few months of persistent prompting from the Holy Spirit that I should indeed write this book, I finally relented, begrudgingly. I have never written a book until now, and definitely did not want to relive the nightmare at my "dream job," as I was still experiencing PTSD. And most importantly, I wanted to minimize any possibility of more retaliation, baseless accusations, threats, harassment, or other potential hits to my reputation. But God gave me the supernatural courage to take the first step, and before I knew it, I had a general outline and two chapters completed. And here we are.

I would also like to thank Robert, Schlyce, Catherine, Nathan, and Dubb for all of the theological upgrades. Your help, patience, friendship, encouragement, and mentorship on my journey was priceless, and I will be forever grateful.

To all of those who supported me, you have my undying respect, gratitude, and loyalty. I never realized how hard it could be to have courage to stand for the truth when the pressure to fold can be so intense.

Lastly, for my accuser. You are a force to be reckoned with. My hope and prayer is that God dramatically changes you from the inside out, and that you become a force for good. May you find the peace, satisfaction, and acceptance that you have always been looking for in the Kingdom—but preferably far away from me, of course.

ENDORSEMENTS

The author has done a fantastic job of tackling a difficult topic. With his unique passion for truth and justice, paired with the authority and authenticity of his own story, *Redemptive Justice* is a must-read for anyone who has been wrongfully accused of sexual misconduct. Freedom lies within its pages.

- **Dubb Alexander**, Author of *From the Cult to the Kingdom*

Redemptive Justice is an honest and informative account of one man's journey of being falsely accused of sexual misconduct. This story will keep its readers turning the pages as he recounts his worst nightmare through an emotional process of learning to trust Jesus and the guidance of the Holy Spirit. This story will inspire hope and the ability to truly forgive no matter what the circumstances look like. The author also includes practical advice and tools to help guide the reader through any kind of injustice.

- **Crystal Derksen**, EFT Practitioner & Mind Renewal Coach and Author of *How to Feel Better Now*

Every now and again, someone writes a powerful book that meets a need in our world, that no one has or is really addressing. The author of this book has masterfully done that. This author boldly goes where few will travel. I found it healing and refreshing for my own soul. I too have been horribly falsely accused, slandered, gossiped, and judged. While I have healed, I found myself healing some more as I read this book. Too long the falsely accused have sat in silent desperation at wounds not of their own making or accord, walking and living in quiet agony at the hands of judges and critics who pronounce guilt before all the facts are in. This author skillfully takes us through his journey with the hope of the power of Christ to be our defender and to bind our broken hearts. His brutal honesty is refreshing in a world of political correctness for those that have been touched with this nightmare. If that were not enough, he goes on to lay out a plan not only of healing, but also of wholeness and life after the carnage. This is a must-read for all leaders. Not one of us that is doing anything worth doing has come through the journey unscathed. This book offers hope for you, and maybe someone you know, who has been through this hell. It is a viable and valuable resource that will stand the test of time. I highly endorse this book.

- **Nathan Blouse**, Founder, The Safe Place Ministry

FOREWORD

I first met the author when he started attending the church where I served on the Leadership Team. Right from the start, he stood out as one of the most honorable and trustworthy men I have ever met. His endearing lack of guile was almost as one belonging to a different age when chivalry and personal honor were lauded. This also reflected a man, who in many ways is ahead of this time, pointing to how God is healing his sons to be responsible, strong, unapologetically masculine, and trustworthy men of honor.

When I first heard of an accusation of sexual harassment that had been waged against him, I was floored. This guy—no way! He is the sort of person you could leave the keys to your home, the keys to your car, and your wallet full of cash and find when you came back home that your lawn was mowed, your car was washed, and your wallet was carefully tucked away so no one would molest it. How he treats women is with the most unusual respect and sensitivity. So, the accusation of him sexually harassing a woman, much less a colleague, was ludicrous! He had fallen victim to a dark agenda and a messed up cultural dynamic.

Our society, in its eagerness to legitimately champion women who have been sexually exploited, has created a "guilty until proven innocent" atmosphere for many men, who are trying to navigate the waters of sexuality with honor. The all-too-real epidemic of women being sexually exploited can bring a backlash that overcompensates and causes us to sink into the other ditch—striking at men who are innocent. One abuse cannot justify the other. We overcome evil with good—not evil payback in kind. Indeed, only God is the one who can truly deal in the currency of vengeance. This is His love-redemption of all things; it is too hot for humanity to handle.

With current social movements, between the third wave of feminism, the "me-too movement," a culture that promotes and celebrates a victim mentality, and the attack on masculinity, being a man can feel like a huge liability. No gender wins at the expense of the other. We only win as we champion one another. God has a huge premium for both His sons and His daughters. And He is just and is ultimately the only one who can heal us in all the ways that we harm one another as men and women.

I walked with the author as a friend and helped him navigate treacherous waters as a coach and counselor out of the hell of character assassination and the fallout that cost him professionally and personally. I witnessed incredible vulnerability and bravery in seeking the Lord to not become bitter; but to heal and be vindicated. His journey has taken a lot longer and has cost a lot more than he anticipated. But I believe he would say it was worth it. It has transformed him personally and with his intimacy with God. His willingness to yield to God directly and through godly counsel has propelled him into a new purpose that emanates from deep within. He is a voice for men who have been broadsided with a false accusation of sexual harassment. His story will resonate and will be a beacon for those innocent men who feel utterly alone in their trial. *Redemptive Justice: For the Falsly Accused, You've Already Won* is a truly unique book that gives voice to a whole population who has been caught in the tidal wave of political correctness and back-lash. What do you do if you are innocent, but accused of sexual harassment? These men need voices as well! The wheels of justice for women truly exploited should not mow down the men, who are just trying to keep their heads down and live as honorably as they can.

In his book, the author shares his dramatic story with candor and humor. He gives the reader practical and spiritual insight, as well as action steps to walk out such situations. It will be a much-needed respite for those honorable men caught in the fray of situations they did not create or deserve. If this is you, or someone you know, this book is a must-read. It is a true honor to know him and to support him in this unique and powerful work!

- **Catherine Toon**, MD, Author, Speaker, Coach, Founder & CEO of Imprint & Catherine Toon Ministries

PREFACE

It was March of 2020. I had tired of the winter weather in Chicago and wished I could get away from it all, but I didn't let on. Pastors don't often have the luxury of letting people know that they're tired of snow that has become slush filled with the grit from car exhaust. Winter is lovely in January, and tiresome by March; and as much as I try to "give it to God," my eye yearns for a color other than white and gray—it's an aesthetic thing I can't avoid noticing within myself.

I was sitting in a meeting with the deacons, trying to decide what to do with a windfall. My great-aunt from Joplin, Missouri, had passed away the year before at 102 years of age. To my surprise, she left $6,000 in the name of my church, Cicero Avenue Brethren Community. Her estate was simple and quickly resolved; the check had just cleared, and it was time to decide where to invest it in our modest budget.

"We need to fix the roof over the fellowship hall, just a small patch job," I told the deacons, and they agreed.

"We have a bid for just over four thousand," said Bill.

"I guess we could give some to the soup kitchen," I said.

"Pastor, you've got *the look*," said Mary.

"What look?"

"You look like I felt before I went to Florida last month."

"And how did you feel?"

"The winter blahs. But when we say that, it seems like something you should just be able to grind through, you know?" Mary said.

"But it isn't. Everybody needs a vacation now and then. Even Pastors," said Bill.

"What are you suggesting?"

"We put the remaining $2000 toward the 'conferences and education' budget to send you south to do a mini-sabbatical. South, or west, or wherever you want to go. Provided you can do it on $2000, or chip in a bit of your own cash."

"I don't—"

"Is that a motion?" Mary said. Bill nodded. "I second," Mary said. "All in favor say *aye*."

Six votes for *aye*. It would have been unanimous except that I abstained. But I wanted to cry.

"Thank you, my friends," I said.

"We'll always have the soup kitchen for the next donation," Bill said.

"You're welcome. Have a great time," added Mary.

That's how I ended up taking Amtrak to the Grand Canyon on the ten-day Grand Canyon Discovery vacation package, with stops in Santa Fe, Williams, Grand Canyon National Park, Flagstaff and Sedona. Sure, I chipped in a few hundred dollars, but I knew it would be worth my time.

I wouldn't be doing any ministry. Hallelujah!

Or so I thought. God always has plans to refresh us, and sometimes He even uses us in the process.

I slept a lot between Chicago and Santa Fe. I intended to take in the engrossing countryside of Kansas, but what can I say? Corn and wheat puts me to sleep. I'd be gazing out the window of the train or reading and then I'd wake up feeling guilty that I was sleeping through my vacation. Of course what really mattered was the Grand Canyon. I wasn't going to miss that! That was the whole point. They tell you the Grand Canyon is stunning. Beautiful. Amazing. It is all of that and more.

Standing at the overlook, I was struck again by the wonder of Creation. I looked around, wanting to share the moment with another human, someone to confirm that what my eyes saw was believable.

There was a man nearby. He was holding both hands over his stomach, and stood slightly hunched, as if he might feel ill. I had met him on the train, and in my normal friendly way, I had struck up a conversation about the quality of the food in the dining car—tolerable, we agreed, but not fantastic—and I remembered his name was Marc.

"You all right, Marc?" I asked. He turned to me with tears in his eyes.

"This is what it feels like," he whispered. "Exactly."

"Ah, it's beautiful, isn't it," I said, misunderstanding.

"It is terrifying. The void. The chasm."

"Are you afraid of heights?"

"No," Marc replied. "It's just—life. You know."

"I see," I said, not seeing.

"I can see how it could be nice for you," Marc said, placing his hands on his hips and straightening to his full height. He set his jaw firmly, and I saw a flicker of bravery in his eye. I tend to think of myself as good at reading people, but I hadn't got Marc yet. Only the sense that he was trying to tough it out, whatever it was. Life. You know.

"Yes, to me it's amazing," I said. "Best of all, there's no snow."

"I'll give you that," Marc said.

"Why did you come?"

"Same as you, I suppose. It's cold in Skokie right now. Bitter. Cold. And I just needed to get away for a while."

"Yeah," I said, "I get that." And I thought I did. Even though it isn't usually bitter cold in March, the thought of bitter cold from the harshest part of winter can linger in your mind like a bad dream until the end of May when you live in Chicagoland.

"Enjoy the rest of the tour," Marc said.

"Thanks. You too."

I saw him again at dinner that evening.

"Can I join you?" He asked.

"Yeah, sure, man. Sit down!" I was glad for company. We ate for a few minutes in silence.

"Better than the food on the train," he said with a grin.

"Yeah, for sure," I said. It was the tenderest steak I'd had in a long time; they do steak properly in Arizona.

"I saw you reading the Bible on the train," Marc said. "Or rather, the Bible was in your lap, and you were sleeping."

I shook my head. "I've been tired. But I'm feeling more refreshed now. Maybe I'll make it through ten whole chapters of Leviticus tonight," I said, poking fun at myself.

"You looked peaceful, sleeping there. Well-rested. Exactly what I was looking for when I took this trip, but I still haven't gotten what I wanted. Something told me I should talk to you more. Are you a preacher or something?"

"As a matter of fact, I am. I'm the pastor at Cicero Avenue Brethren Community Church," I said. "And yes, I slept a lot on the train."

"I'm a Christian, too," Marc said.

"Oh, great, always good to meet a brother," I said. I had half a mind to ask him the usual questions—what sort of church do you attend, could you share your testimony, but something held me back. Instead, I said, "What was it, today? When we were looking out over the canyon? What's troubling you?"

"Well, Pastor. I'm scared to go to church. I'm afraid they won't believe my story."

"Try me," I said, "You've got no reason to lie to me. And anyway, I'm happy to offer my professional confidentiality."

"Right. Like I said, something told me I should talk to you. I guess it was God. I was sitting there trying to pray. I felt like I was supposed to take this trip to try to forget about it for a while, but as I was praying, I felt like the Lord said, 'Go up to the observation deck and find a man with the Bible, he'll help you.' And I went up there, and saw you, so I knew it was the Lord, but you were asleep, and I chickened out for a while. I wondered if I was really hearing Him right, even though I saw you and the Bible right there just like He said I would, and . . ." Marc trailed off. "Everything's been hard these days. I question everything, I keep wondering if I'm going crazy, I doubt myself, I doubt God, even when He's about as clear as you could ever hope for. You see, I've been falsely accused of sexual misconduct at work—I mean, harassment. I need help, and I don't know who I can talk to. So, if I could share my story with you, maybe if you'd have some advice . . ."

And I thought I wasn't going to be doing any ministry on this vacation!

Marc and I had many more conversations after that. Long after my vacation was over, I was still working with Marc. But I rarely had advice for him. For the most part, I just listened to his story, and believed what he said. He was able to come up with most of the advice he needed, by digging into scripture for himself.

1 Corinthians 4:5 (AMP):

So do not go on passing judgment before the appointed time, but wait until the Lord comes, for He will both bring to light the [secret] things that are hidden in darkness and disclose the motives of the hearts. Then each one's praise will come from God.

INTRODUCTION

You are not reading this book by accident. If you picked up this book because you have been falsely accused of something, you are not alone. I believe that you were led to this book by divine appointment, just as Marc was led to me. The Holy Spirit got you here, maybe without you even realizing it.

Once Marc started to explain his situation, he wanted to tell me everything; all the details came flooding out. "See, Pastor, once I realized I was being falsely accused of something very serious with grave consequences, it's really been difficult to get off my mind. One minute, you feel like your head is spinning. Thoughts racing through your mind without ceasing, you know? You may feel like anxiety is choking and suffocating you. You might relate to sleep as a dear friend you would like to spend time with again: when I saw you sleeping on the train, I didn't criticize you for falling asleep at reading the Bible, I just felt jealous that you could rest. But it can be worse than that, sometimes. You may feel like fear is covering you like a blanket, making it hard to see and hear and think about what God is saying in His still small voice. You try to focus. You may even feel fear screaming at you: "God can't save you! God won't save you! Your life is ruined! Your life is over! Forget about your dreams! Just give up, you can't win anyway! No one will ever listen to you! No one believes you! Nobody cares about you! Your life doesn't matter! It is hopeless to fight! Have you considered suicide?" He stopped, clapped his hand over his mouth.

"Have you?"

"It's the voices, mostly," he said. "I tell them no, it's not an option. I'm not making those kinds of plans."

"All right," I said, "let's go on. But I want to make sure you have a hotline number." I grabbed my phone and googled it. "The National Suicide Prevention Lifeline, 1-800-273-8255. 'After July 16, 2022, you can dial 988 to get the same lifeline.' Remember that: 988." I wrote it on a scrap of paper and asked Marc to put it in his wallet.

Much later, when it was all over, Marc emailed me. He said, "I have been there. I know what it feels like to live under the death sentence of a false accusation. I remember how it felt to have hopelessness invade my life and felt powerless to evict it. I know what it is like to feel your world permanently turned upside down by a complete lie, a false accusation that took just mere moments to make. This is beyond hard. This is completely unfair. This is stunning. This is incapacitating. This is terrifying. This seems insurmountable. It seems like there is no end in sight. This is a real life nightmare you cannot just wake up from, relieved it was just a dream."

But the good news in Marc's case, is that by the Grace of God, he not only survived the ordeal and came out clean, but now Marc has used the pain of the experience to transform his life into a life of purpose. Although I did not consider myself an expert on overcoming a false accusation, I saw a man who needed help. As he began to pull back the curtain on all the events, I also began to pray for strength, because advocating for someone in this kind of threatening life circumstance takes wisdom, too.

Perhaps you're a pastor as well, or a counselor. Perhaps you picked up this book because you'd like to know how to help a friend. Maybe you're married to someone who has been falsely accused. Whether you came to this book as someone who has been falsely accused of any kind of misconduct or as someone who will try to help another along the journey, we have a story to tell, Marc's story. A story of how God helped Marc untangle himself from a web of lies and deceit, and use spiritual weapons to overcome the real enemy, Satan. Marc's story is a story of God never leaving him nor forsaking him, and rescuing him against all odds. For the odds truly are against you if you've been accused of sexual harassment: in the #MeToo era it is tantamount to a career death sentence. In fact, in today's politically charged climate, anything regarding sexual misconduct has become the new lightning rod for scrutiny, with political pressure to act quickly and believe the victim, and not the accused, no matter what. Regardless of the facts, most of the time, the accused is judged as guilty without even a hint of consideration that the accusation might not be true. *Due process—what is that? An unbiased investigation—why bother? No one would ever falsely accuse someone of sexual misconduct. That is absurd! Why would anyone ever make something like that up?* For most decent people, who understand the ruin it can inflict, it is inconceivable to do something like that! Why? For spite? Decent people might feel jealous of someone, or spiteful, but they'd never stoop that low, and it's hard to imagine that someone would play this sort of deadly game. And if that is the case, then the next logical step is that the verdict is clear and has already been decided. The accused has to be guilty! And if they even attempt to defend themselves, eyes roll, insults are hurled, and they get scoffed at any time they try to plead their case. It's as if no one wants to listen to them, much less believe them. The jury has made their decision before the trial ever got started. I think about the courage that it took for Marc to approach me, just a random pastor on a train, knowing that I might easily fall into this camp of decent, fair-minded folk who would have trouble imagining that someone could do this. In Marc's mind, it was likely that I'd side with his accuser before he could talk for three minutes. It's funny. We have no trouble imagining that someone would murder someone else. Or commit adultery. But when it comes to making a false accusation, the fact that the world is full of true accusations of all sorts of crime and wrongdoing, confuses the issue.

It's so easy to jump to the conclusion that you are a liar and a coward, a monster who preys on innocent, defenseless women; our media has taught us for decades that these monsters are legion: rapists, predators, molesters, and all kinds of deviant sex addicts. It requires no thinking. But . . . what if you aren't the liar? What if you aren't the monster? What if there are people out there who enjoy victimizing others by playing the victim themselves? What do you do when the one who is scary, cunning, and manipulative isn't the one who is accused—it's the accuser? Who knew that there was an art to acting like a battered or abused victim? It is so darn easy to be believable! And for the falsely accused, who is in their corner? Where is their advocate? They are left alone, seeing the stunning hypocrisy unfolding before them like a horror film without the ability to turn it off.

"I'm so grateful I had you, Pastor. Thank you again, just for listening to my story without judging me." Marc wrote in his email.

If the scenario I am describing is hitting way too close to home, take heart. A new day is here. Consider this book as a sign from Heaven. The Lord is shining His face upon you and turning the tables on what the enemy had planned for you. You are not alone. There is at least one person alive on this planet who is standing with you on the side of truth—me! In fact, I took on the project of writing this book as direct instruction from the Lord. I believe the Lord is going to get you through this! I believe Jesus is going to rescue you! If he can do it for Marc, He can do it for you. God does not show partiality,[1] and I cannot wait to hear your story of how God saved you!

---

[1] Acts 10:34

Even as I write these words, I feel the Lord speaking to me about you and your situation. I can see you and the Lord inside what seems like a spherical invisible force-field bubble, impervious to the arrows coming at you from all directions. You and Jesus are walking through the treacherous maze of your circumstances unscathed. Friend, Jesus is the best GPS you could possibly have. He is going to lead you through this, helping you maneuver through each twist and turn at the right time and right place. He sent me as a witness to this truth and to tell you this—Jesus wants you to let Him take care of this problem for you! And I truly believe reading this book will help!

Take a few deep breaths . . . breathe in the Breath of Life . . . and exhale God's presence . . .

Relax . . . God has got this!

Chapter One
America, We Have an Integrity Problem

The first one to plead his case seems right,
until another comes and cross-examines him.
- Proverbs 18:17 (AMP)

After I met Marc, I began to research prominent American cases of alleged sexual misconduct, as well as alleged physical, mental and sexual abuse. As I mentioned in the introduction, there are many cases where the sexual misconduct charge turns up a guilty verdict. This only adds to the confusion when someone is innocent. Men (and women, too) are fallen creatures and are notorious for doing horrible things to one another. We know our own hearts, with our own capacity for lascivious thoughts. We guard ourselves against these behaviors, and therefore it is easy to see how others, just a little bit less guarded, could end up doing something awful.

Indeed, after all the publicity surrounding the cases where the charges led to guilty verdicts, it's harder for most people to imagine that someone would be upright and innocent. But I believed Marc's story. Marc was not alone; false accusations have a long and sordid history.

BRETT KAVANAUGH

You would have had to be living under a rock to escape the controversy surrounding the Brett Kavanaugh hearings. They not only riveted our nation, they brought the issue of false accusations directly into the spotlight and into living rooms throughout the entire country, if not the world. On one side of the issue was Brett Kavanaugh, a man many of his peers considered to be of great intellect in the field of law, as well as a man of good moral character. To those who knew him personally, testimony showed he is considered to not only be a good father, but a good husband, as well. Up to that point in his life, he had never been thought of as a man who participated in sexual misconduct, sexual harassment, rape, or any other nefarious act. But yet here he was, on the cusp of nomination, when seemingly out of nowhere there came a very serious accusation of rape by Christine Ford. Obviously, this was stunning for him and his family. It was embarrassing as well, given the hard conversations he would have to have with his daughters about what rape meant, and why these people were saying bad things about their Dad. One can only imagine the bewilderment his daughters must have felt, to realize that people were accusing their dad of rape.

Regardless of your convictions politically, the Brett Kavanaugh hearings were one of the most public examples in recent history of the current political climate where a mere accusation was considered a verdict of guilt. This was a scenario where due process was not given due course. People are judged guilty before the facts are verified, and careers and reputations are train wrecked with uncorroborated testimony. There is a certain stigma attached to accusations of sexual misconduct that follow the accused for life—a modern-day scarlet letter. In the Brett Kavanaugh situation, the press had a relentless heyday with this story. Although in the end Christine Ford was proven to be an inconsistent witness, and Judge Kavanaugh was ultimately confirmed to the Supreme Court, irreparable damage was done. Despite different versions of events of the accuser's testimony when compared to the testimony from other witnesses and factual timelines, nothing happened to Christine Ford, other than profiting from her six figure GoFundMe account. People can say Kavanaugh turned out okay, but that entire process left a mark on him and his family. It is shameful what happened not only to Kavanaugh, but also to the decorum of ethics in American government as well.

DUKE LACROSSE PLAYERS

Remember the Duke Lacrosse Case? When I first saw it on TV many years ago, I just felt in my gut when the allegations first hit national news that there was more to the story than was put forth by the media. Back in 2006, this was a widely reported criminal case in which three members of the Duke Lacrosse Men's Team were falsely accused of rape, and the rush to judgement had those three players all but convicted in the court of public opinion. Their professors publicly stated they thought they were guilty. Students on campus held rallies protesting the alleged event. This one had it all: racism, rape, privilege that comes with money, media bias, along with a malicious prosecutor who later was disbarred due to misconduct.

An African American female college student (not a Duke University college student), worked as a stripper. She falsely accused three Caucasian male students on the Lacrosse team of raping her at a house party that other members of the team were attending one night.

What ensued was a travesty. The District Attorney not only wanted to prosecute the players for rape, but also for a hate crime.

The Duke Lacrosse Coach was forced to resign, and the season was cancelled by the university. This team was poised to compete for the national championship, as they were ranked #1 at the time, and lost the national championship game the prior year by one score. The coach left and found employment elsewhere. Some of the players transferred to another school to get away from the stigma of being associated as a Lacrosse player at Duke. A lot of people had to deal with unfair circumstances, all stemming from a false accusation of rape.

The North Carolina Attorney General finally stepped in. The District Attorney was disbarred for dishonesty and fraud regarding DNA testing, and also went to jail, albeit for one day. The charges against the falsely accused Duke Lacrosse players were finally dropped. I remember the Attorney General on TV saying they were completely exonerated. Afterwards, it was discovered that the District Attorney was up for re-election and was pandering for votes to appear tough on crime, but was hypocritically willing to commit a crime himself, as he was willing to sacrifice the lives of three young men in the process by being dishonest with DNA testing. People bring all kinds of ulterior motives to these cases, and political jockeying is not the least of those motives.

Those Duke Lacrosse players experienced the injustice that ensues from a false accusation. And their accuser faced no criminal charges for her dishonesty. Her false accusation set in motion many events that negatively impacted others to a great degree, putting those three Duke lacrosse players, in particular, in a great amount of peril, and nothing happened to her. Incredible how someone can get away with that, isn't it?

MALE HIGH SCHOOL TEACHER IN OKLAHOMA

In this story, the accused man was both an entrepreneur and part-time faculty at a local high school. He owned a $500K per year photography business, taught photography, and coached soccer at the high school. A sixteen-year-old female student accused him of sexual contact both at his home and at school. To his surprise and humiliation, he was arrested at school and escorted out in police custody. Due to the nature of the alleged crime, he was immediately placed in solitary confinement to protect him from the general population in prison. This lasted for ninety days. He was only allowed one hour per day of daylight, and was locked in a small room without windows for the rest. Before the arrest, he was not aware that the teenage girl had been making these wild accusations.

When accusations like this arise, sometimes a lot of people pile on, and want to see people destroyed. During those long ninety days, he was fired from the school. His wife bought into the lie and quickly divorced him. His business went bankrupt. And to make matters worse, he received death threats from his fellow prisoners.

Fortunately for him, an older brother of a student he taught was an inmate in the local prison. This man had a lot of authority with the prison inmates, and after discovering that this high school teacher was in the same prison, he protected him from anyone meaning him harm. Why did he extend this kind gesture and protect him? Well, this teacher helped his younger brother at the school. He was kind and patient with this student, and genuinely cared about him. This younger brother apparently bragged a lot to his older brother during visitation of how great a teacher and coach he was— the best! When you do something simple, like treating a person like a human being with worth and value, isn't it amazing how that can sometimes pay huge dividends later down the road?!

When the accused was in solitary confinement, he had a chance to collect himself after his life completely unraveled in mere moments. He finally decided to pray and ask the Lord for His help. Although estranged from his stepfather, he felt like he should reach out and make a call. His stepfather hired one the best attorneys in the state. Needless to say, this whole process brought him and his stepfather much closer.

In the end, this man was supernaturally exonerated and released from prison. As it turns out, that sixteen-year-old girl couldn't keep her story straight on the stand. The judge promptly dismissed the case. The judge pointed at the girl and said that she should be ashamed of herself. That was the extent of her punishment.

This fired coach was a good man but had to defend himself from a false accusation at much cost—everything, really. Although the case was dismissed, his reputation was ruined, and he lost everything. It adds insult to injury that there were no repercussions for the sixteen-year-old girl. That story broke my heart. It is egregiously wrong on every level. Of note, after all that was over, his wife, or should I say ex-wife, met with him a few times and apologized tearfully. But by then, it was far too late for their marriage.

The silver lining in this story is that he grew very close to God during that time. God gave him the grace to forgive. He felt like he was not supposed to pursue legal action for restitution or to seek justice for the wrongs that happened to him. So he graciously relocated and moved on with his life and pursued other entrepreneurial endeavors in another state.

I first heard this story back in 2015, even before I met Marc, and to this day, it is still both heart-breaking and infuriating with how a false accusation can destroy a good man's life, just like that. I am beyond impressed with this man, and he deserves much honor. He is a one in a million to have the supernatural grace to move on from something so bad that cost him everything. I hope he has a lot of treasure in Heaven, and I hope the Lord abundantly blesses him beyond his wildest dreams while he is on this Earth. This man is gold in my book and always will be.

MALE HIGH SCHOOL STUDENT IN PENNSYLVANIA

I kept digging; the stories kept coming. Here is another sad story; perhaps if you are in the middle of your own case it could feel difficult to read any more of these stories. Feel free to skip ahead but know that the point is to share with the world that these false accusation cases are more common than most people realize. You are not alone.

This story involves an innocent male high school student in Pennsylvania, along with a group of "mean girls," a reference to a 2004 movie with that title. A group of girls decided they "just don't like him," and made not one, but two, false accusations of sexual assault.[2] This male student had a summer job as a lifeguard. One of the mean girls began conspiring with the others to get him fired. She falsely accused him of sexual assault at the pool. Unfortunately, that plan worked—he was promptly fired.

When school started in the fall, another girl decided to tell a school counselor that this male student sexually assaulted her at her home. The second girl was coached by the first accuser. Of note, this male student was invited to a party at that very home. Because of these accusations, he was bullied at the school—some even put tape on his back that said "PREDATOR."

This male student was ultimately charged and was removed from school in shackles. He then spent nine days in juvenile detention. Next, he was released on house arrest wearing an ankle bracelet. He could not leave the house, unless to attend church, or to attend psychological therapy, due to the emotional trauma of having his life turned upside down from these false accusations. He was not

---

[2] www.dailymail.co.uk High School clique of five 'mean girls' are sued for targeting a boy with false sexual assault allegations because they 'just don't like him' by Kayla Brantley

allowed to play baseball with his teammates at the high school as well.

Fortunately, the conspiracy started to unravel later that school year. Other students came forward contradicting the accusations from the mean girls. The girls begrudgingly admitted their lies. "I just don't like him." "I just don't like to hear him talk." "I don't like to look at him." "I would do anything to get him expelled." These are direct quotes. All charges were dropped and his record was expunged. But nothing happened to the Mean Girls. Shameful! The family of that male student has filed a lawsuit against the school, the parents of the mean girls, and the district attorney. Good for him! I hope he gets justice. And I hope more people going through this type of hell start pushing back.

You can see that I am torn. The high school teacher didn't retaliate, and I called him gracious. But this boy filed a counter-lawsuit, and I applauded him. I have come to recognize that there's a problem in our society, where there is no justice for those who perpetrate a false accusation, no matter whether their reason is political, driven by jealousy, or because they simply don't like the way a boy talks or looks.

Ultimately, if you have been falsely accused and are acquitted, you will have to decide for yourself whether or not filing some kind of countersuit is right for you. That is between you and the Father. Some people will choose to do so, and be victorious, so that laws can change, and repercussions increase. Others will decide that this isn't their battle; that their battle is to graciously move on. Still others, like Marc, will share their stories and invite others to advocate for the falsely accused in books like this.

There are different ways to stand up for yourself when you've been falsely accused. Jesus said that the truth will set you free, and you will be free indeed.[3] For some, freedom means moving to another state and graciously starting over. For others, freedom means firing back in court; our nation does have laws that allow this, and citizens do have the freedom to a countersuit. Still others find that telling their story in a book or from whatever pulpit they find is a way to reclaim their freedom.

ME TOO

This next one literally made me laugh out loud, not because of "rape," but because of the stunning level of hypocrisy. Asia Argento, an actress who was one of the first to champion the #Me Too movement and was one of the first women to accuse Harvey Weinstein (a now defamed former movie mogul) of rape, has later admitted to having a sexual relationship with an underage male. I was not able to find any legal ramifications for Argento, but I would assume that is because this story does not fit the narratives that drive media sales.

MALE COLLEGE STUDENT IN CALIFORNIA

Here is another story that took place at the University of California-Davis, regarding a male student that was accused of sexual misconduct. The male student and a female student had a class together. One night they kissed and touched each other with their clothes on, both consensually and mutually, according to the accusing female's statement. She had a hickey from that encounter, and afterward felt self-conscious and embarrassed about it. Later that same night, she told him that he should have asked for permission before touching her, although she didn't ask for permission while she was touching him.

After much cajoling from her mother, insisting that she was violated and ought to do something about it, she reported him for

---

[3] John 8:32,36

sexual misconduct to the university. He received an email from the university, informing him that he was the subject of an investigation for alleged sexual assault. His family then procured an attorney for legal representation. In the end, the University found him "not responsible" on the basis that the female student had indicated consent. He and his family did not have a lot of money, but ultimately spent nearly a year's worth of tuition to defend him against an allegation of sexual misconduct that, in the end was determined to be consensual—she merely changed her mind about their romantic encounter after the fact. Although she gave indication of her consent at the time (according to her statement), she later became upset and started to feel uncomfortable about their encounter.

It is disappointing that it is so costly to defend yourself against something so frivolous. Fortunately, the female student did not appeal, dragging this nightmare out further. She did not spend a dime.

GUY IN COLORADO

I found this next story a little scary. Before we begin, I am not advocating the moral merits of this story, but simply pointing out what a mere allegation can do to a person. The accused was a Christian man, by the way, but let's face it, people have sex outside marriage all the time, including those who claim to be Christians. This story involved a guy in his mid-twenties meeting a woman in a bar, also in her mid-twenties. They hit it off, had drinks, and decided they would go to her place to have sex. However, they were so drunk that they never actually had sex. Upon awakening, she accused him of rape. He insisted that wasn't true, as they were both too drunk to have sex and actually slept all night in bed. I would have to presume that this was not the good morning he expected, right?! She called the police and he was arrested. He was brought in for questioning. The District Attorney came in and laid out the charges and options.

Option 1 was go to trial and then go to prison for 16 years if convicted. *Option 2* was a plea deal and his sentence would be reduced to 4 years in prison with no trial. Both options would leave him with a criminal record as a felon, along with registering as a sex offender. Not many good future options after that, right?! The District Attorney only cared about getting a conviction, not whether he was innocent or guilty. Keep in mind that all of this happened in less than twenty-four hours since he first met the woman. His head was spinning in complete disbelief. Neither option was good, obviously, but he was getting intimidated to accept a plea deal for something he did not do. He finally was able to talk to an attorney. He again insisted that he definitely did not rape her, as they never had sex in the first place, but he was also scared of going to prison for 16 years. The attorney's guidance was to fight this in court, as the facts would come out during the case. Fortunately for him, he was found not guilty. The attorney allowed him to pay the legal bills on a payment plan that was spread over 5 years, like a car loan, and he was thankful for every payment he made. He was obviously relieved and thankful for the outcome, but he had post-traumatic stress disorder from that incident, as I am sure most would. Since then, he stays in his apartment while not working, as he is too afraid to socially interact with others. He would like one day to get married and have kids, like most do, but is way too scared to ask out a lady on a date to get know her. What a terrible, sad situation! I hope and pray this guy meets someone special and can have the kind of life he has hoped and dreamed of.

A BETTER WAY

Why are people in authority, whether school administrators, employers, law enforcement, or prosecutors, focused on favoring females who are doing the accusing while dismissing the accused males? For much of history, women were afraid to say anything when they were abused. Over the last century, in many parts of the world, the pendulum has swung in the other direction, as we have championed women who had the courage to step forward and say it: "I was raped." "He touched me." "He texted me unsolicited dirty pictures." No longer is the victim shamed. It allows women who have been hurt to bring their trauma to the light and seek justice. But this wave of social change bears with it a worrisome contrasting development. The mantra of "believe women" or "believe survivors" ignores the possibility of false accusations. I believe former President Trump was correct, when he said that it is a "scary time for young men in America." It is time to reexamine defamation laws in this country!

I believe victims of sex crimes need to be treated with respect and heard by the authorities, but they do not have the right to be believed without question. As you can see, an accusation does not equal the truth. Sometimes an alleged victim is not the victim. Sometimes the accused is the victim.

The #MeToo movement has affected every sector of society. I am glad there is a movement to protect our women from the horrors of sexual abuse. But there is also another movement afoot. There are many women out there who see the vileness of false accusations from women ruining the lives of innocent men. They don't want to see their father or husband or brother or son get bullied and pushed around by political correctness, and an eager legal system ready to prosecute, with district attorneys making their political careers on convictions. Many women are using the hashtag #ProtectOurBoys and #MenToo, along with https://helpsaveoursons.com, to denounce what they consider false accusations. I was glad to discover that.

Women need men. And men need women. We are attracted to one another, and we ought to be, as we were created to be attractive and attracted. God created us to be partners, not adversaries. God created us to love and respect each other. Our society needs safe ways to indicate our attraction and interest in getting to know another person. I encourage you not to believe the lie that the other gender is the enemy. You have an enemy. He is the devil. "Your adversary, the devil, prowls around like a roaring lion, seeking someone to devour." [4]

I encourage you to do what Jesus told us to do, "Treat others the same way you want them to treat you."[5] We need to be asking a lot of specific questions around this as a society, to protect men and women alike: How would you like others to indicate their attraction to you? What is the best way to treat others at a party? How would you like to be treated when you've had two or more drinks? What are the things that will make us feel regret and shame when the chips have fallen, and the dust has cleared? How can we protect women when they have been hurt, taking their accusation seriously? At the same time, how can we ensure that men aren't destroyed by vicious women who have found ways to manipulate a system suddenly conducive to their guile?

If we all followed Christ's Golden Rule, we really could have world peace.

---

[4] 1 Peter 5:8, NASB
[5] Luke 6:31, AMP

I encourage you to do what Jesus told us to do, "Treat others the same way you want them to treat you."

Chapter Two
The Accusation

————————————

Marc and I sat there in the restaurant, and he began to unload his story. I remember that when Marc told me he'd been accused of sexual misconduct, my steak suddenly lost its flavor. Now I realized why Marc was holding his stomach as we looked over the Grand Canyon. It's a man's worst nightmare. Even hearing about it makes you feel that you've been punched in the stomach . . . or below the belt. It knocks the wind out of you.

The second thing that happens is you are tempted to decide whether you believe the guy, without hearing any more information. I sat back and told myself to relax and hear what he had to say. I could reserve judgment.

"You feel like you could confide in me, Marc, and it is clear that the Lord led you to me. He wants me to listen. Go ahead and tell me your story," I said.

"It was only a few weeks ago, on February 10, 2020," he said, "the day my life changed forever. I knew it immediately. Felt it in my gut. I'm a dentist, and you know, there's a kind of cracking sound when you pull a tooth, a very unique sound. It's that sort of sensation, like someone is forcibly breaking you away from where you've been rooted. You have these questions, like, am I rotten? But I'm not! It's a complete fabrication. It was like, you're pulling the wrong tooth."

"Oh, yeah, that would be bad," I said.

"Exactly. That day, my dream job became a nightmare. I was away from work, welcoming a much-needed break from the drama. I started receiving text messages from some coworkers warning me to get an attorney. I was told that I was not only being of accused of sexual harassment, but I was going to be legally charged with those allegations. I sat down, looking at these texts, thinking, 'What just happened?' That's not the kind of thing co-workers joke about. We joke about pulling the wrong tooth, not sexual harassment lawsuits. In my spirit, I immediately discerned that they were telling me the truth and that this was very serious. I was in complete awe that my accuser would take things this far in her quest for revenge. I was in a state of panic!"

"Back up a second," I said. "She's after revenge, I get that, but before you go on, tell me: what kind of guy would you say you are?"

"Me?" said Marc, "Well, I would characterize myself as a rule-following, smart, risk-averse man with a sense of duty to do the right thing. I like to think I have a witty sense of humor as well. I am amiable, but I'm definitely not a womanizer. I am a Christian, hopefully a good one; I mean, I'm actively following Jesus. I attend church and home Bible studies. Although I was never a member of the Boy Scouts, people sometimes called me one. In my late teens and early twenties, some of my friends said I was 'every parent's dream.' This was because I did not drink alcohol. I did not smoke cigarettes. I did not go around having sex, as I wanted to save my virginity until I was married. I certainly did not do drugs. Clean record—no criminality. Good reputation. I didn't rebel. I worked hard at school. Pre-Med major. Graduated with honors. Went to school full-time and worked part-time for five years to get my bachelor's degree. I then left home and went away to school for four more years to become a dentist, with another two years after that for a residency. I was one week shy of twenty-nine when my education and training was finally over. It was at that time that I finally entered the workforce and started my career.

"I remember attending many trainings through the years about sexual harassment. During those trainings, I remember thinking, 'I have never done that!' or 'I don't do that!' or 'Doing that has never entered my mind! If I just continue with what I have always done, then I will be fine.' Until that day in February of 2020, I honestly never thought I would be accused of sexual harassment, because I would never give anyone a reason to make an accusation.

"From ages 29-34, I was not in a financial position to be married, so therefore I felt in my heart trying to pursue a woman to marry was impractical and unwise. I suppose that also means I had not met the right one yet. But I finally met the woman of my dreams and got engaged at thirty-five when I was on the cusp of having my student loan debt paid off in full—living like you are still a poor college student can really help reduce principal, you know. During our relationship, we decided we would not kiss until the day of our wedding ceremony, literally waiting until the pastor gave me permission to kiss the bride. I realize that may sound naïve and impractical, but nevertheless, that was our decision and how we wanted do things. Unfortunately, things did not work out with her . . . or maybe I should say, with her family. The mother-in-law-to-be was a looming presence in the relationship—well, to say the least. Let's leave it at that. This failed engagement is perhaps the biggest disappointment of my life. And I suppose it would be fair to say that I still feel disappointment about it to this day."

"I'm sorry," I said, "sounds like a hard decision to break that off." Marc nodded. He thought for a moment, then continued.

"And here I am at age 44, still never-married and saving my virginity, being accused of sexual harassment. Again, I am a rule-follower, and I took the weekly drumbeat in church youth group of 'no premarital sex' to heart. I am the antithesis of someone that would sexually harass anyone. In fact, I had a female coworker about five years older than me, another dentist . . . just last week, she told me that of all the people she has ever worked with in her career, that she considered me to be the least likely person to ever sexually harass anyone. It's nice to know there are other women at work who see me for who I really am, but I don't know how this is going to play out. I sure hope someone like her is willing to testify. I really don't know how it works yet. She also said that nobody else believed my accuser and that everyone knew I had integrity and wouldn't do that. I truly appreciated that; I knew she was trying to encourage me. I would guess that ninety-nine percent of my co-workers don't believe my accuser, but we are the mere proletariat. The one percent in charge, however, well, it seems they bought the lie. Hook, line, and sinker. This was only a few weeks ago and now, even though so many of my coworkers know it's false, it looks like I'm going to have a rough go of it. But that is the irony of it all. A dark irony: the union, Human Resources, and Management chose a side—my accuser's side. They actually did more than choose a side, it was like they're married to the idea that my accuser is the victim, and I am the bad guy who needs to go down."

"Look, Marc," I said, "I don't know you from Adam, but from what you're saying, this is almost unbelievable. Not that I don't believe you—" I added quickly, "But who in their right mind would accuse anyone who is such a 'Boy Scout'?"

"Well," he said, "Let me give you a little background about my accuser. Maybe it will make a bit more sense. I'll call her, um, 'Melissa'," he said.

"At the time of her hiring, Melissa was a divorced woman, I'd say early thirties. No kids. Has a couple of pets. Makes a great first impression. Charming. Confident. Charismatic. Smart. Capable. Likable. Good Dentist."

"What's not to like?" I asked.

Marc nodded. "Yeah, Pastor. That is what I thought, too . . . at first. Well, I know now that she is twisted and devious. It's kind of hard to be devious if you appear evil from the outset. You have to start with a good impression, or the schemes don't work later on. I think she is a wicked, recalcitrant reprobate who will stop at nothing to get her way. She's terrifying. She even bragged about being a narcissistic sociopath. Look that up, it's scary."

"Those are some whopping dictionary words right there," I said. "Recalcitrant reprobate?"

"It means—"

"I know what it means, it's just that most people would call her the B-word and be done with it—"

"I'm a Boy-Scout type, remember?" said Marc, with a wry smile. "And I've been thinking about it a lot. The thesaurus in my head has been working overtime trying to find words to describe her; words that aren't the B-word."

"Fair enough," I said. "We'll go with recalcitrant reprobate."

"Anyway," he continued, "Although I am no psychiatrist, based on my experience with her already, I can confidently say that I concur with her self-diagnosis. She's frightening and my gut says that this whole mess she caused could be devastating.

"Anyways, this is what I know about her so far: Melissa boasts that she prefers her boyfriends to be rich or super-rich, worth at least a couple million if not tens of millions; they have to be lean, fit, married guys with silver hair, they don't do much but manage portfolios and work out, usually members of the Chicago Yacht Club; guys who will take her shopping on Michigan Avenue, drop a few thousand on clothes and shoes, and then take her out sailing on the lake, or better yet deep-sea fishing off Florida or Mexico. To other people at work, she brags about using cocaine with her boyfriends and she thinks it's hilarious to wreck marriages, it's almost like she's notching divorces on her belt or something. Honestly, I'm a little surprised none of those wives have come after her, but maybe they're just more interested in getting their half of the cash, I don't know.

"I've seen it myself. She openly hates authority. Openly hates men, unless they are 'hot' —by which she usually means rich. Her skirts she wears to work are shorter than her lab jacket, her blouses are cut so low you'd think she was auditioning for Hooter's or something. Somebody texted me the other day and said that a patient's wife even complained that she was trying to flirt with her husband, like she was tugging at her shirt to show extra cleavage. This was all while the patient's wife was sitting next to him! The more I find out, the more shocked I become with her behavior. I keep thinking she couldn't shock me any more, then I realize that's her thing: pushing the edge of authority to see how much she can get away with, flaunting and flirting her way through life."

"Wow," I said, "It's amazing that management would ever consider that you were the one in the wrong, especially if they're getting complaints from patients' spouses."

"Thanks, Pastor, I appreciate your belief in me. That's why I was scared and embarrassed to go to church. You know, they all know me, and they have since I was a kid. They've watched me go through my engagement and breakup with integrity, but you know, these days, everything is hyper-sexualized, and people believe that men's minds are dirty, always thinking about sex. I'm worried that they're all secretly wondering when the other shoe will drop, you know?"

"It's going to be tough going through this without support," I said, "But I can appreciate why you wanted to talk about it with someone virtually anonymous."

"Yeah. Like, you don't know my last name."

"Right," I said. "Well, here's my card, feel free to call and make an appointment. I want to stay in touch, and I'll support you however I can."

"Thanks, Pastor."

Marc and I had to get on with our trip. But over the coming weeks and months Marc learned more about the other key players in his case, and would call with updates.

A few weeks went by, when I got such a call from Marc.

"Hey Pastor. Well, I got a little background about the union president, let's just call her 'Rebecca,' and it isn't looking good. She is pretty much a soul mate to Melissa, and it seems they've become close friends. They call each other Missy and Becky, as if they've been BFFs since fourth grade. Rebecca is a party girl, likes to go to raves and dance all night with college girls. Some hygienists said that she would sometimes report to work stoned or high on something harder. She is not loyal, she has no allegiance to anyone but herself. A well-known backstabber. I heard her mentor is very high up in the union on a national level, and Rebecca is not one to be trifled with.

"The title of *Union President* comes with a lot of power and access. Rebecca can talk to executive leadership on a moment's notice. Executive leadership and senior management, per the contract, have to get approval from the union president on pretty much everything. I have witnessed members of executive leadership calling Rebecca to get approval on things several times. Organizationally speaking, she has the same level as the top executive in terms of power and authority, but on the labor side of the organizational chart. But it seems to me as though Rebecca has the most power, as they have to pretty much run everything by her. For Melissa, having the help of the union president is no small matter. On the other hand, having the union president slander you to management and executive leadership is also no small matter. So, in my case, Rebecca siding with Melissa is a big deal.

"Up until now, I honestly thought that a union president ought to be thought of as a friend for employees—not best friends, going-to-happy-hour-after- work type of deal, but a friend at work that can keep confidences. Rebecca is someone who is supposed to advocate for me, or at least be impartial between me and Melissa. And indeed, I did have a good relationship with Rebecca. She used to come into my office on occasion asking me how I was doing, sometimes came to me to vent and cry about her frustrations, etc. Again, I thought we were friends, and I had no reason to believe otherwise."

I learned from Marc that in the weeks leading up to his false accusation, he had been ignorant of Melissa and Rebecca's budding friendship. He found out later they went partying and clubbing together, did lines of cocaine together, and even planned a trip outside the country together. During their time together as best friends, Dental personnel were omitted from the random drug screening list. To this day, Marc has no idea how Rebecca pulled that off, but my suspicion is that management knew why games were being played. Rebecca was conveniently not obliged to random drug screenings herself. Soon enough we found that Marc was up against people who were used to getting their way.

The interesting thing about their friendship was the dynamic. Although Rebecca was very powerful, it appeared that Melissa was the alpha mean girl in the relationship. Rebecca followed her lead. At times, it seemed as though Melissa had permission to speak on her behalf. The union president is an elected position; there were times Marc thought Melissa was planning to subterfuge her way into becoming the next union president, by undermining her own best buddy.

THE SITUATION

"So, Marc," I said one day, "I get that Melissa is the kind of person who would do this to anyone, if she felt like she could take some advantage of a situation to her own benefit." He nodded.

"But why you?" I couldn't really understand why a nice guy like Marc had become a target. But that's like asking why someone on a gravel road in the middle of nowhere uses a stop sign for target practice. The answer, as I discovered, is no more complicated than that stop sign is something to shoot at.

Marc was the Coordinator for the Dental Student Program, as assigned by the Dental Supervisor. He explained how the mess had started.

"I let Melissa help teach the students due to her past experience elsewhere and went along with her insistence to get involved as a preceptor. I'm a nice guy, and never thought that someone would angle to get me eliminated so they could have my job! One day, I'd say a couple of semesters after I allowed her to assist me in the Student Program, I could not help but overhear two male students excited about attending a rave party with Melissa on a Friday night. The conversation was a few feet from my office door, which was open. By that time, I found Melissa to be volatile and unpredictable, so I never felt comfortable about broaching the topic of fraternizing with the students, as they were unpaid interns in a subordinate relationship to her. I was already intimidated by her and did not want her trying to teach me a lesson. I could only imagine what she'd do, but I knew if I rubbed her the wrong way, she'd do something.

"As time went on, I noticed Melissa was taking a tremendous liking to one of the male students in particular. Things started becoming optional for this student, like coming to the office on time or doing testing he did not like to do because it was 'boring.' There were many one-on-one teaching moments behind closed doors for that student with her, some for unusually long periods of time. By the way they interacted with each other, it seemed they had become close. My suspicions continued to grow about the possibility of this student and her having a personal non-working relationship likely involving sex, but again, I never felt comfortable having a discussion regarding the ethical merits of having a relationship with a student, as I was truly afraid of the wrath that would follow."

"But wasn't she working under you in teaching these students? You said that you allowed her to help teach."

"True," Marc said, "But I also was not her supervisor, I was just running the Student Program. Because I grew increasingly more wary of her, I thought it would be prudent to mind my own business, and that is exactly what I did. Maybe her tastes weren't limited to rich guys with silver hair and yachts. Or maybe that student came from a family with money, I don't know. But she did whatever she wanted, that seemed to be the way of it. My comfort level of sharing the same work area with her decreased by the day, to the point I did not feel safe at all. I discussed my concerns at least once a month with my supervisor, and even requested to transfer to another location, which meant doubling my commute, one hour to work and one hour home. My discernment was on high alert, and I even mentioned to my supervisor that I was scared of any possible false allegations from her. Looking back on it, I feel the Holy Spirit was warning me to leave. During that time, I actually had another fantastic unsolicited offer for employment elsewhere, but I unfortunately over-thought the situation and did not follow my gut instincts. I guess I was too cautious. Wow, did I regret that!"

THE INEVITABLE CALL

Marc looked at me and sighed.

"You know, Pastor, sometimes it's the smallest promptings that we don't pick up on right away. It's hard not to blame yourself."

"Sure," I said. "The Lord gives us free will, sometimes figuring out what is a suggestion and what requires obedience is tricky. So, what happened next?"

"The following Semester," Marc continued, "I received a call from the Clinical Director at the University one late Friday afternoon. They were having concerns, as gossip seemed to have reached them a thousand miles away. He told me that they have heard rumors that 'my' female dentist, who was teaching 'their' male students, was not only having sexual relationships with the male students, but there was drug use as well. Did you notice the school said "students"—plural? Well, there you have it. We had a ginormous problem! What I remember as odd about the conversation, other than the obvious, was that he was more fearful that the dean would find out and wanted to get ahead of the situation but was less concerned about the awkwardness around the morality of the situation. I was speechless. My pause of silence had to be very loud coming through the phone on his end. He informed me that he was coming for a site visit the following month, which was something that had never happened before. He insisted that she was my problem and not the school's problem. I was in the middle, as he did not feel comfortable discussing this issue with my supervisor. He made sure to let me know it was my problem.

"As soon as I got off the phone, I walked to my supervisor's office, Dr. Davis, and notified her. She told me that she didn't want to have anything to do with this, so she told me to notify her supervisor, that is, the senior manager, Mr. Smith."

"Dr. Davis just passed the buck?"

"Yeah, great leadership there, Dr. Davis," Marc said, his voice dripping with bitter sarcasm, "but perhaps that was her self-preservation instinct kicking in."

"Yeah, I get that," I said, "seems like your supervisor didn't want to be the responsible one here."

"Pretty much," Marc said, "But I was honestly relieved, too, as Mr. Smith seemed like the only adult in the building that was in management. At this point, there was no official whistle blowing, and there never really was. I was just very concerned and worried, and I just wanted guidance from management on exactly what they wanted me to do. Surely, they wanted something done, right?! Although this was new territory for me, the answer seemed obvious on how to fix this situation. But I did not want to presume, so I let Mr. Smith come to the obvious conclusion on his own."

"And he didn't fire her? What, did Mr. Smith not care at all?"

"No—no," Marc said. "Thankfully, Mr. Smith was appalled! I should have insisted on written approval, but he told me to immediately remove Melissa from the Student Program and insisted I do it before the weekend began. He did not feel the need to discuss this with the University, as they were not employees. He was about to transfer in less than a month, so looking back on it, I wonder if that made him more courageous and assertive. I truly felt horrible about notifying Melissa that she was no longer part of the teaching team, and I never went into why, but the look in her eyes told me that she was very angry about hearing the news—well, more than angry, more like I-will-make-you-regret-ever-living kind of fury. I just knew by the steely resolve in her eyes that she was not going to let this go, and that she was going to defiantly insist on getting her status back as a preceptor for the Student Program. I suspected she would even insist on having me removed as the Student Coordinator so she could be that herself instead. And as events unfolded, that gut instinct I had proved to be right."

Marc stopped and shook his head. I could see he was still wishing he had followed the Holy Spirit's prompting to leave when he had that offer. I knew he was feeling some regret about that, but I trusted that he would learn and the Lord would make something good come out of his bad situation, so I waited to see what would happen next. He sighed and continued.

"Indeed, that was one of her objectives in her quest for revenge. The following Monday morning, Melissa and the union president, Rebecca, had a closed door meeting that lasted over an hour. Scheduled patient appointments ran behind and all. I was surprised that meeting hadn't already taken place at one of their houses over the weekend, but they wasted very little time before they decided to get back at me.

"Come to find out, that meeting they had was to plot their retaliation and my demise, while keeping Melissa out of trouble. The plan was to manufacture and gather "evidence" while having me secretly investigated, and surprise me on short notice for an interview to wrap up the "investigation." But fortunately, I had friends warn me via text messages to prepare for what was coming in February."

"So, all that happened before things really hit the fan," I said.

"Yes, and it really would have blindsided me, too. But it is hard to keep an investigation a secret when someone like Melissa is prancing around the clinic saying I would be fired and brought up on criminal charges of sexual harassment. I am glad she couldn't keep her mouth shut; it gave me time to prepare."

"This just gets crazier and crazier," I said. "What kind of help did you get from Mr. Smith?"

"I guess Melissa intimidated everyone, you know, all the way to the top. Mr. Smith, who was initially appalled about the activity with the students, quickly backtracked and denied ever giving me verbal permission to remove her from the Student Program as preceptor. Again, I should have insisted on written permission, like an email or something, anything I could print. As it turned out, he was afraid of Rebecca, like everyone else. His tone changed, as he started asking me if I have ever been inappropriate with my accuser."

"What?" I said. "Didn't everyone know you're a clean-cut guy?"

"Yeah, I know," Marc said, "The week before, he was appalled and gave me permission to remove her from the Student Program due inappropriate sexual relationships and drug use with the students, and now I am the suspicious bad guy?! Unbelievable! Melissa and Rebecca got to him and convinced him to see things from their perspective."

"So, there you have it, Pastor. My reward for doing the right thing and removing a preceptor who was behaving unethically with students? Retaliation in the form of a false accusation of sexual harassment! I had no support from Management, nor Human Resources, and certainly not from the union or the university. Wow! I couldn't believe this was happening! It was like Judgement Day looming over my head, and let's just say I did not feel like I was going to be raptured! It was doom for me. You know in the movies when they're standing on a trapdoor and all of a sudden it opens up and they're falling? Well, that's me."

My discernment was on high alert, and I even mentioned to my supervisor that I was scared of any possible false allegations from her. Looking back on it, I feel the Holy Spirit was warning me to leave.

Chapter Three
The Investigation

As you can see from the stories I shared, along with Marc's story thus far, it's evident that false accusations of sexual misconduct are more common than people realize, and they are very serious. But I did not pay close attention to them until I met Marc during a time when a false accusation was turning his life upside down. Sure, I had seen cases of alleged sexual misconduct occasionally on the news, but it wasn't until it impacted someone I knew personally, that I really understood the devastation that happens when someone chooses to falsely accuse you of something terrible.

Marc's nightmare became even worse when new management arrived. Mr. Smith was about to transfer to another location. He was initially appalled by the behavior of Marc's accuser until he backed down. Eventually, Mr. Smith finally left and was replaced by another person, Mr. Richardson. By the time Mr. Richardson was on duty as senior manager, he had already been briefed about Marc's sexual harassment investigation. I saw that Marc had no opportunity to develop a relationship or rapport with Mr. Richardson. Melissa had already set things in motion, with the help and assistance of Rebecca, the Union President.

"Shouldn't the union be supporting you?" I asked Marc. "What's their job supposed to be here? I mean, you pay monthly dues, right? The person you demoted has a complaint, but you're both union members, right? How can they not be impartial?"

"Sure. You would think there would be some way to deal fairly between two union members, right? Rebecca had weekly meetings with senior management and executive leadership as part of her duties. Apparently, my name was frequently an agenda item. Both management and the union were decidedly against me, but for Melissa. Well, me and God. But thank goodness that the God living in me is greater than corrupt management and union officials in the world!"

That was Marc on a good day, when he wasn't depressed about his situation.

Later, Marc found out that Rebecca was telling new management that he was a serial sexual harasser. The accusation had expanded from not just Melissa, but now that he sexually harassed Rebecca, too! Yes, Marc, the rule-following, virgin Boy Scout dentist who follows orders and never complains. I remember one time when we debriefed, after the whole thing was over, it turned out that things were worse than Marc could have imagined:

"Although my gut was telling me that I was unfairly being perceived by Mr. Richardson, I was completely unaware of exactly how bad things were behind the scenes. Apparently, my charismatic accuser was rallying new management to her cause. Everything was going against me."

—————————————

I remember another conversation Marc and I had over coffee in the middle of the investigation.

"How are you doing, brother?" I asked.

"It's really tough right now, Pastor. My imagination is in overdrive. I try to stay positive, but I'm tormented! All I can think about is the worst-case scenario: felony conviction, registered sex offender, jail time, my state license to practice will never be renewed, I'll be unable to find housing or a new job. If not in jail, I'm sure I'll be homeless. All this torment over what?! A lie?! Something that never happened?! Death would be better than this!"

I knew I needed to keep tabs on Marc daily.

"Suicide isn't the way out," I said. "You still have that hotline number I gave you?"

"No, I know. Yes, I have it. But it is surreal. Like a dream. But unfortunately, this is a real-life nightmare. You know when you're in a nightmare and you think, I wish I could wake up? And yet your subconscious has you trapped asleep? It's horrible."

NEW SENIOR MANAGER

After Marc's first senior manager finally transferred, his successor, Mr. Richardson, was on board ready for duty the following week. It wasn't an improvement for Marc.

"From what I heard, Mr. Smith could not leave fast enough. Unfortunately, this new senior manager could not possibly be a worse fit for me. Pastor, you're not going to believe this. He told me, 'I have no problem with her having sex with students, as long as it is consensual and not on business time.' What?! He clearly was not appalled, not even concerned. I was stunned he said that with such conviction. 'But what about on business property?' I asked. He appeared to not like that question. He stammered and stuttered his way through the rest of the conversation, trying to make the excuse that the students were consenting adults. This guy was said to be from a strict, disciplined background, as he was a former Marine, and I was beyond shocked he seemed to support or at least tolerate having a dentist fraternizing with unpaid student interns. Just hanging out on weekends could create conflicts of interest, let alone having casual sex with them."

"That's odd," I said, wondering aloud, "what's in it for him? Is he getting threatened that he'd be next to get accused?"

"Pastor, I don't like to listen to rumors, but right now I have to have my ear to the ground. Rumors are swirling in the clinic that he and my accuser are having sex, too."

"Already? Wow, if these rumors are true, Melissa is going after everybody. If they're clean, she accuses them of being dirty; if they're dirty, she has sex with them. Are you sure it's a good idea to listen to rumors?"

"Look, don't judge me, Pastor," he said. "I've prayed about it. You know how the scripture says to be as wise as a serpent and innocent as a dove?"[6]

"Yes," I said.

Marc shrugged. "Well, I got the innocent part down, but the serpent is low to the ground. He keeps his eyes out so he doesn't get his head stepped on. Look, I don't know what to do. Everybody does what Melissa wants them to do. Except me. And look where it's gotten me so far. I can't prove that they're having sex, but we've all seen them together in public and anyone will tell you they're acting familiar. Half a dozen of us saw Melissa and Mr. Richardson walking out the door at the end of the day together. A few colleagues confided in me that they saw the the two of them at a bar later on

---

[6] Matthew 10:16

that evening and he had his arm around her waist, so, ..." Marc shrugged.

"It doesn't matter," he said. "The point is, it's me against the world."

"Welcome to the Christian life," I said. "Except, it isn't just you. Let's pray together that the Father will watch over you, because this situation is volatile and if there's anything I'm hearing loud and clear, the only people at work who would support you are the ones with the least power."

NOT LOOKING GOOD

The weeks went by; I continued to meet with Marc once or twice a week. Nobody at my church minded. We were a small church, but a healthy one, and my schedule wasn't as packed as most pastors' schedules are. I was careful not to judge Marc, and just be a sounding board, someone he could talk to when he felt overwhelmed. And I truly liked the guy. The more time I spent with him the more his own description of his character rang true. Soon, Marc was out of options. He went from being a well-liked and respected dentist at work, to becoming toxic and radioactive overnight. Despite multiple attempts, neither management or Human Resources would respond to his requests for meetings so he could plead his case. In spite of his years of earning the highest ratings possible on his evaluations, along with zero documented patient complaints, none of that history mattered. Although Rebecca had a fiduciary responsibility to him, she blocked union representation and protection. Marc didn't trust her, but he wanted to get her on record.

"No one at work will listen to me," he said. "Everyone is listening to Melissa and treating her like a celebrity. I feel so alone. I still have some friends who want to help; they know I am innocent, but they either don't know what to do or they're too afraid to intervene. I feel like a gazelle getting pounced upon by a pride of lions on the Serengeti. The other gazelles are sorry to see this happen to me, but what tools do gazelles have to help one of their own when he's being ripped to shreds? They are just thankful it isn't happening to them. They've started to distance themselves from me, and take shelter in their offices whenever I walk by."

"You'd think they know that if the culture doesn't change, it's coming their way eventually," I said.

We worked together, but it was hard to watch. Anxiety and fear were suffocating Marc. He couldn't sleep. When we met, I saw the bags under his eyes. He said that some days he didn't eat at all, but whenever we got coffee together what I saw was that he ate way too much. Donuts. He'd get a dozen, say he was going to take them to work, and when we were done with our early-morning coffee time, sometimes he'd look down and realize that he'd eaten about half of them. He gained 40 pounds, then stopped eating because he was so nervous, and lost 25, then gained another 30 on top of that!

"You know I'm concerned," I said.

"Man, Pastor. It's way too difficult to concentrate at work. Daily panic attacks . . . we work in the same area. Melissa's office is just four doors down the hall. She leaves her door open, I can hear her bragging and chatting it up with people all day."

"It's taking a toll. I can see that you're miserable," I said.

"It's horrendous. She terrorizes me every day," he said, with tears in his eyes. We kept praying.

I never understood why management thought it was a good idea to keep the two of them working in such close proximity. But Marc had to persist. If he bailed on his job, he'd only look guilty.

A NEW HOPE

Much later, Marc told me that it took him a while to realize that his only option was to ask God for help. He was out of options . . .

except for one. Funny how sometimes we don't think of that first! But Marc was so traumatized and in shock, that he wasn't thinking clearly. Looking back, I think the bitterness he was experiencing delayed him reaching out to the church for help. Out of options, he took a vacation. He thought about throwing himself into the Grand Canyon.

"You know," he said, "it was the Spirit prompting me when I saw you with that Bible. And later, when you looked at me with compassion. I guess you thought I felt sick to my stomach, maybe something I ate."

I knew it was embarrassing for him to share what he was going through, but Marc desperately needed help, hope, and a strategy for a path forward. After he began talking to me, he was also able to share with his Bible study at church and they began to support him as well. He did get encouragement from prayer and prophetic words that he would be fine, bringing fleeting moments of peace. But often, fear and doubt and anxiety would creep in, and Marc would be overwhelmed by the "what ifs" that came in like a tsunami crushing the fragile peace he occasionally had.

"It was a truly miserable experience!" He said later. "But breakthrough finally came. I had an epiphany! Truth will be my defense! Imagine that!"

After I gave him some advice, and he heard from others in his church, too, Marc began to put together a notebook of timelines, evidence, statements from others, photos from social media, etc. Marc became something of a sleuth and told me that sometimes he even enjoyed running his own mini spy operation. I had a hunch this notebook would be the turning point; I encouraged Marc to make several copies.

THE 180

Finally, in December of 2020, Marc called me.

"Hey Pastor, guess what?!"

"Um," I said, wondering if all the charges had been dropped.

"After months of being 'secretly' investigated, with my accuser making daily proclamations that I am going down and all, they're finally going to do the interrogation today!"

"How are you feeling?" I asked.

"Believe it or not, I am relieved. I just want closure!"

"When is it?" I asked.

"At noon," he said.

I looked at my watch—10:30 a.m.

"I am ready! I can't wait to shed the truth on this situation. I am going all in and I'm not backing down!"

"Gonna stand your ground?" I said, thinking of Tom Petty and the Heartbreakers.

"I have the truth on my side, and I am not bluffing! You know what else is crazy? I was assigned a union representative a few days ago. The preparation for the upcoming interrogation was underwhelming, to say the least. I may have mentioned that I might bring a notebook of evidence supporting my claims. I asked if I could have an attorney present instead, as I did not see the benefit of having this union help me. They said no."

But surprise, surprise! At the meeting, Marc had discovered that Melissa was allowed to bring an attorney for her interview sessions, in addition to union representation. The double standard never ceased to amaze me!

"What happened?" I asked Marc when I called him that evening.

"The investigator seemed like a very organized individual. He arrived early, prepared seating arrangements, had his computer and recording device ready, notepad out with what seemed like way too many writing utensils on standby. I was sure each one had a purpose, with the care and attention to lay them down at precise locations. I almost "accidentally" bumped the table to watch those writing utensils roll and careen off the table. I was feeling feisty, I guess, but discretion and the Holy Spirit got the better of me, thankfully. I sat down at my assigned seat, ready to start, with not one but two notebooks beside me—I had that copy you suggested. The investigator was glancing over at my notebooks but seemed to not want me catch him doing that. I looked him in the eye the whole time."

We later found out that almost nobody brings those types of things to a "fact-finding interview." Marc suspects, and I concur, that the intent was not for this to be a normal fact-finding interview, but a mere formality to complete a witch hunt investigation with the outcome already predetermined.

"You went in with courage and truth on your side, and evidence," I said.

"Right. Little did I know that this investigator was about to commit a faux pas. He pressed the button on his recording device and started the interrogation. He starts with basic stuff, like state your name, position and title, duration of employment, etc. Then everything abruptly changed. He started asking me if I have ever made sexual advances toward Melissa, or if I ever touched her inappropriately, etc. I'm sure you get the point. The tone of his voice and the look in his eyes told me he was 100% convinced I was guilty.

"My union representative, the one assigned just a few days ago, finally showed up about ten to fifteen minutes late. As soon as he walked through the door, they started barking at each other. The recording device was turned off, and the interrogation came to a grinding halt. I was sitting there wondering what the heck is going on. As it turned out, that faux pas by the investigator was starting the interrogation without union representation present. Although I gave verbal consent to start the interrogation without a union representative, according to the contract, a fact-finding interview is not to ensue without a union representative there, regardless of whether I agreed or not. The investigator knew that, but I didn't. But let's face it, it was not as though I had a lot of confidence in the union to support me. During the short break, the investigator called executive leadership and Human Resources, while the union representative called the union president. I put both notebooks in my backpack and stepped out."

"Smart, you didn't want to let those notebooks out of your sight, right?" I asked.

"Right. So, then the investigation turned completely in my favor at the point when I turned in that divinely-inspired notebook. The investigator pressed the record button again and resumed the interrogation. It was at that moment that I pulled out the notebook and gave him a copy. Timing is everything, right?! When I gave the notebook to the investigator, he verbalized receiving it and voiced his displeasure for causing him more work, all on tape with a union representative present! The investigator thought he had this all wrapped up, with me being the last interview. He acted incredulous when he realized I was prepared to defend myself. I know, the audacity of me trying to defend myself, right?! When I gave the investigator the notebook, I could tell he knew I was serious, and that I had the resolve to take this all the way. I made him promise me that he would read it."

"And this was all being recorded with your union representative present?"

"Even a kangaroo court has to have a witness," Marc said. "I told him, 'When you read that, I think you will find I am not the villain in this story.' As far as I am concerned, anyone who has the nerve to falsely accuse someone of something serious as sexual misconduct, fully knowing the ramifications that it causes for the accused, needs to be exposed for the liars that they are! And that was my aim, in addition to proving my innocence!

"Meanwhile, from the other side of that large building, I could start to hear the striking of stilettos against the tile floor getting closer. Rebecca stormed in and told everyone to leave, except she wanted the investigator to stay so she could educate him. I walked out and stood there in the hallway. Door slams. Screaming and shouting, with the blood curdling decibels coming from Rebecca. Door slams again. Rebecca stormed out of the office with tears in her eyes, but this time, no indignant stare down from her. Checkmate. Rebecca apparently was aware I had some sort of evidence file, and she was on the prowl to stop it. But it was too late. The investigator told her to pound sand and kept the notebook. As a courtesy, I then gave a copy to the union representative as well."

From what Marc heard later, that investigator was impressed with the outrageous and salacious content of the notebook, and made another copy for himself, so he could work from home and make notes and write reports. I guess at least one person decided to do their job.

Although the investigation was far from over, it was at that point Marc and I both knew he had won. We thanked the Lord together!

Soon, Melissa and Rebecca would be exposed as liars trying to ruin an innocent man's reputation. That close friendship they were enjoying quickly changed after much finger pointing. Within a couple of weeks, they were enemies!

Marc found out later, the union did a parallel investigation, independent of the investigation conducted by executive leadership and Human Resources. There were now two competing investigations, and I said, "Marc, we have to assume the union president knew that there would likely be two different findings. No wonder she was so upset about your notebook!" I told him I thought she was scared that she and her friend were about to get exposed. The investigation the union did was already completed and turned in before the investigation by management concluded.

––––––––––––

"What gets me to this very day, Pastor," Marc said a couple of years after the fact, "was their willingness to let an innocent and good man's life be ruined over a bold lie, doubling down at every opportunity. It was amazing how much peril I was in, through no fault of my own. And just to be clear, if investigation findings did uncover 'evidence' of sexual harassment, my professional state board would have been notified, along with a referral to the Attorney General's Office. This was no small matter. They were trying to create a state-wide scandal with me, all for the sheer embarrassment of it all. Competing claims matter as well, as investigators can use discretion if they see fit to choose a side that is more believable. Want to know something else that wasn't fair about all of this? Up to that point the investigator only interviewed people who could corroborate Melissa's story, not mine. The fix was in. That investigation had a predetermined outcome with the goal of trying to prove my malfeasance, and I am beyond thankful that the Lord saved me from their evil plan!"

As you can well imagine, when Marc turned in that notebook, it set in motion months of more investigations, but this time, Marc wasn't the subject. There were many findings from all those investigations, but one finding uncovered a "mean girls" club, with Melissa as its leader. A group of women from various departments, including Dental, apparently made a pact to accuse people they did not like of something nefarious and the rest would rally to the "victim" and corroborate the accuser's story, with the goal of getting their target demoted and/or fired. They would notify Rebecca, who would notify management, which usually meant an investigation was going to happen.

Well, mean girls are sometimes mean to each other. "There was a literal argument that escalated to hair being pulled, and slaps and punches landed, in the break room one day," Marc said. He had become "wise as a serpent" while continuing to be innocent as a dove. He had paid attention to rumors enough so that he wouldn't get blindsided again. "To this day, I have never found out what that argument was about, but it must have been pretty bad, because there were plenty of other sordid things, examples of mean girls being mean to one another, that had not escalated to fisticuffs. Again, given the outrageousness of everything going on at this place, the rumors seemed very believable."

"Well, Marc," I said, "I guess when people do hurtful things in concert, it eventually deteriorates into every mean girl for herself, huh? So, you don't know what the boxing match was about?"

"No," he said, "I don't know. But whatever the disagreement was about, one of the mean girls, the one who was assaulted by Melissa, she was out for blood and turned on them all. She basically verified everything that I said during the investigation (and for months prior, as I was completely ignored), along with what was also in the notebook I turned in. Ha! Isn't God great or what?! I was cleared. I was told through back channels that I was clean. Someone told me they heard the investigator say, "We got nothing on him."

"Did you do anything to get this other mean girl to rat out the rest of them for their lies?" I asked, curious if Marc had found a supporter on the inside due to his own cunning.

"I never talked with her, we never became friends, nor did she see my evidence-filled notebook. I did not coach her or corroborate with her on what to say. How could I? I don't really know her. She spilled the beans on her own accord, which proved I was telling the truth all along. Another finding from that investigation was that they determined they had gotten "less than candor" from Melissa—a very polite way of saying she was lying.

"Now these investigators I met had a weird, morbid desire for satisfaction that could only be fulfilled by doling out harsh discipline of the career-ending variety. For them to say I was clean was remarkable, as they were originally married to the idea that I was guilty. And for them to do a 180-degree change of opinion about me was a miracle! Thank God!"

THE FALLOUT

Not much happened to the mean girls, other than the metaphorical slapping of the wrists. Melissa was transferred to another location where careers go to die, with the obvious added benefit to Marc of finally having her separated from him in the workplace. She saw the writing on the wall and left the company about a year later. Also, about a year later, Rebecca was investigated for embezzling funds. She was later indicted and went to prison. The Department of Labor received a "tip." This union president seemed to burn every bridge she made with people.

"What on earth was in that notebook?" I asked Marc one day as the fallout continued.

"God blessed me with a source who heard what was happening to me and felt compelled to reach out and point me in the right direction. This source knew where the skeletons were hidden. Apparently, union dues helped finance personal trips for Rebecca, and there was a paper trail that showed how she'd been able to go to Cancun six times in one year, while she was supposedly at 'conferences.' Oops!

"It was great to know what I turned in uncovered a systemic conspiracy of the mean girls falsely accusing their 'enemies' of whatever suited them at the time. I thought and hoped that management would congratulate me on how I helped bring things to light. I honestly thought everything would go back to normal, and that management would view me as a trustworthy and valued employee again. I was naïve. On the contrary, management was more determined than ever to find something on me. You might be fortunate enough to win a battle, but they will never let you win a war. I won the first round, not realizing there would be more. I guess winning a fight with me was more important than the actual truth. I was actually warned before defending myself from these false accusations, that the people I was defending myself from were 'evil and vindictive' and that I should consider finding employment elsewhere. Again, perhaps I should have taken that fantastic unsolicited job offer.

"It baffles me to this day on how I, a mere dentist among hundreds of employees, became so important to management."

"Why not? This seems like a pretty big deal to me," I said.

"Management had lots of other issues they were dealing with. It was the Wild West in our health care system, Pastor. We had patients committing suicide in the bathroom, cases where lazy care had caused bad outcomes leading to negligence lawsuits, employee's cars vandalized in the employee parking lot, narcotics missing from the pharmacy, years of forged peer review signatures by a department head, and even an employee who embezzled over a million dollars that were earmarked for patient home care. It's crazy. You go into a huge health care system and on the surface, everything seems so professional. And it's not like everyone's doing a terrible job. It just takes a few bad apples. And there are hundreds of employees."

After Marc was finally cleared of sexual harassment there were yet more investigations of the administrative variety regarding bylaws and policies, as the bureaucracy tried to get him on a technicality. I didn't need to watch television, I just met with Marc a couple of times every week. Goodness, the drama. Law-fare at its finest! Melissa still had friends in management even after she left, and there were still ongoing attempts to set Marc up and play the gotcha game. The baton was passed so that someone else could make his life difficult. These additional investigations were very serious as well, but long story short, findings did not uncover any issues.

One day we met for coffee. Marc was still struggling with his weight gain. We live in a real world, and even when we pray together and trust in the Lord, the stress is like a cold, hard gun pressed against the back of your head.

"Still more investigations?" I asked, bewildered for my friend.

"Administrative headaches," he said. "You know, Pastor, I stood my ground through the worst of it. I have had enough. This is never going to stop unless I leave. And I'm not backing out as a coward. It's my choice, I'm taking control of my own future now."

So, Marc raised the white flag with his head held high. He had won his most important battle and decided he didn't want to spend the rest of his career in a war zone. It was January of 2022 when he resigned, and I'd been meeting with him a few times a week, for near two years. There were days when I saw that the Spirit was giving him peace, but the many months of being harassed and persecuted and under unfair investigation beat all the ambition and optimism and determination out of him. Marc was exhausted not only emotionally, but physically as well. He was a dentist. He could get a job anywhere, but when he quit, he called me up and said, "I did it. I'm out."

"How do you feel?" I asked him.

"You know, Pastor," he said, "I ought to get on that train and go back to the Grand Canyon. I feel like I could sleep non-stop for a year. I'll take my Bible and put it on my lap and sleep all the way through Kansas and Oklahoma, just like you did. I just want to be left alone."

SILVER LINING

Marc's dream job had turned into a nightmare. The position he had been selected for was very competitive and coveted by peers all over the country—applicants were capped at 200 during a two-week window, and he was the only one selected!

"I am thankful that I am no longer in that toxic work environment, and that I am in a safe and stable place to continue my restoration and healing from those incredibly traumatic events. This also gave me opportunity to get direction from the Lord on what my purpose is, along with what I am really supposed to be doing with advancing His Kingdom. So, there was ultimately a good outcome from all of this. I now realize my purpose and am living out my "why," which is not Dentistry."

Marc and I had discussed this whole topic of having a *why*. I shared with him my *why* as a pastor: I believe everyone should have one really good friend who can listen to their problems without judging them.

"I sure needed that when I met you!" Marc said, laughing.

What is a *why*, you ask? It is simply your God-given purpose and destiny for living. What God had in mind when He made you. Your *why* is what makes you want to enthusiastically get out of bed in the morning and live life to the fullest. Your *why* is what gets you energized.

"I would have never discovered my *why* if this horrible experience hadn't happened," Marc said. "But because of it, I know that my *why* is to bring bullies to justice and hold them accountable, so that their victims can be rescued and restored.

"God has rescued me and is still in the process of restoring me. After my experience at my "dream job," my eyes have been opened to a whole world of injustice from false accusations. I now easily identify with people who have been falsely accused, harassed, persecuted, and bullied. I identify with people who can't defend themselves, with people that are being bullied to such an egregious degree that suicide seems like the only way out, as they have no more hope left. I will now forever want to know the other side of the story. These are the people I feel called to help, and I know God wants to help them more than I."

"What do you wish you could tell them, Marc?" I asked. "What would you want people who are being falsely accused, persecuted, and bullied to know?"

"God cares for you. His heart is to give hope to the hopeless, and to set the captives free. He told us this in Isaiah 61:1, and Jesus said it, too, in Luke 4:18. He is there to rescue you, to restore you, to put your feet on the Rock so you can partner with God with building His Kingdom. God wants you to know that you are not alone. God loves you more than you can imagine. God does not want you to agree with the lies and judgements said about you, but to agree with what God says about you. God convicts you of His righteousness,[7] not the bad things the devil wants to condemn you of. God wants the best for you. God really can save you and rescue you. God can turn everything around for you in a day. With God, anything is possible![8] Don't lose hope!"

"I couldn't have preached a better sermon myself, Marc," I said, smiling at him.

I could see the relief on his face. It was over. All things come to an end.

"Really?" He said. "Thanks!"

"You've never heard me preach," I said, "we only visit during the early mornings, on weekdays."

"And you think I preach better than you?"

"Look, I'm good at listening," I said. "Not every pastor is a good preacher. What can I say? People fall asleep when I preach."

"Ha," Marc said, "You even put yourself to sleep sometimes."

---

[7] John 16:8-11
[8] Matthew 19:26

With God, anything is possible!
Don't lose hope!

Chapter Four
Find Your Tribe

Hi everyone. This is now me, Marc, speaking. I asked the pastor to write out the first part of my story for me. He's been able to bring his objectivity to the topic, and I appreciate that a lot. He took plenty of notes—maybe not a full notebook like I did, but he followed my case and helped me put into words what needed to be said about my case. The Pastor was a huge part of my "tribe," and I want to share with you about how important that is.

"You need to preach that sermon; *you* write it, Marc," he said as we sat there sipping our coffee at 5:00 a.m. one Wednesday. He took out a package. It was gift wrapped.

"Happy Birthday," he said.

"It's not my birthday," I said.

"I don't know when it is, but Happy Birthday anyway."

I opened the package. It was a brand-new notebook, with a package of pens.

"So, from now on instead of taking notes like a crime scene investigator, you can take notes about the sermons God is giving you to preach," he said.

"Wow. Thanks. Thanks for everything, Pastor." I flipped open the first page. "Who should I preach to first?" I wondered. Then I just began to write:

If you are falsely accused or bullied at work . . .

YOU ARE NOT ALONE

If you are reading this book because you or a loved one has been falsely accused, I want you to know that you are not alone. It sucks, and I know that firsthand. I also know that you know deep down that this is a huge problem that you just can't ignore. There are grave implications. This may be the fight of your life. Some of the things I'll share in the following chapters I knew before the whole false accusation thing happened; I was a Christian a long time before any of this went down, and you'd think I would have been prepared. And in many ways, I was. But I also learned how to apply what I knew, and I was learning from the Pastor and others who walked along side me as I went through the ordeal, too. That's important. I had people with me, and I kept learning.

So, before we dig in, take a deep breath. Say it aloud: "I am not alone."

Have you ever heard the saying, "There are no atheists in the foxhole!?" I have heard that several times in my life, whether in movies, or from people using a metaphor to describe a dire situation. A foxhole is a literal hole that is dug into the ground by soldiers and used to provide cover against enemy fire, or as a place to fire back. So, in times of great stress and fear, such as during war or fighting back against a serious false accusation, people will naturally hope for and believe in God, the most powerful Person in the Universe, to rescue and protect them. In this foxhole you are in, just know that you are not alone. There are three names you can call on at any time: Jesus, Holy Spirit, and Papa.

Papa is one of the names I have heard other Christians use for the Heavenly Father. If you study the Bible seriously, you'll see that Jesus called the Heavenly Father *Abba* when he was on the cross, which translates closely to "Papa," and I happen to like it.[9] I have also heard *Dad* and *Heavenly Dad*, *Daddy* and *Heavenly Daddy*, and *Father God*; I think you should use whatever you feel brings you closer to Him.

Know that they are there with you. In fact, the triune God is not only with you, He is on your side and He wants to fight this battle for you. Trust me when I say that. I speak from experience. If you'll let Him, God Almighty, the Creator of the Universe will lead your defense team. He will also surround you with other people, a tribe if you will, that will go the distance with you. It doesn't matter what your relationship with God looks like today. If you are ready to go deeper, God will not only bring you through this situation to victory, but your relationship with Him will never be the same. Let's talk a bit about these three people, this tight-knit family, who are with you in the Foxhole. Who are they? Make sure you have a Bible handy so that you can read some of the verses I'm going to suggest, and even read a few lines before and after if you want, to get the context around the message.

JESUS—THE CAPTAIN OF YOUR SALVATION

Jesus said that He would be with you always (remaining with you perpetually—regardless of circumstance, and on every

---

[9] Mark 14:36

occasion), even to the end.[10] So, Jesus will always be there with you, even to the end of this journey.

Jesus also said that you would have tribulation and distress and suffering in the world, but to be courageous (confident, undaunted, filled with joy) because Jesus has overcome the world.[11] Because Jesus has overcome the trouble in the world for you, in your case a false accusation, you can be confident and joyful in the outcome.

Additionally, Jesus said through the writer of Hebrews that He will never (under any circumstances) desert you (nor give you up nor leave you without support, nor will leave you helpless) nor will forsake you or let you down. So you can take comfort, be encouraged, and confidently say that the Lord is your Helper (in time of need). You will not be afraid. What can man to do you?[12] Let that sink in. Jesus will never forsake you or let you down! Awesome! Jesus is the most reliable person you could possibly know!

To recap those verses, Jesus will be with you while you are having trouble with this false accusation, you need not worry and can be courageous, as Jesus has already overcome this false accusation for you! Jesus will never leave you! Isn't that encouraging? During my journey of overcoming a false accusation, there were plenty of people in my workplace who abandoned me to keep their head down and avoid getting caught in the crossfire. Those verses gave me encouragement and hope that Jesus was with me and had my back, and that Jesus would rescue me from being falsely accused. And Jesus will do the same for you! Jesus was in the foxhole with me, and there was no way I was going to be an atheist.

---

[10] Matthew 28:20, AMP
[11] John 16:33, AMP
[12] Heberews 13:5-6, AMP

HOLY SPIRIT—THE SPIRIT OF TRUTH

Jesus also gave you the Holy Spirit (Helper, Comforter, Advocate, Intercessor, Counselor, Strengthener) to be in close fellowship with you.[13] I just love those different names for the Holy Spirit. The Holy Spirit definitely helped me, comforted me, advocated for me, counseled me, strengthened me, and gave me fellowship when I was on my journey. The Holy Spirit will do the same for you too! I am so thankful the Holy Spirit was with me and did all the heavy lifting for me. Imagine being in a foxhole, bullets flying over your head, but there's someone who has an incredible ability to comfort you. Your panic recedes. A calmness rules supreme in your heart, in your gut. You are able to relax, even sleep, while you're under fire. Thank you, Holy Spirit!

FATHER GOD—YOUR DEFENDER

As a Christian, you are baptized (immersed) in Father God, Jesus, and the Holy Spirit.[14]

Father God loves you. He gave you His Son Jesus so that you can have eternal life.[15]

Father God promised the Holy Spirit to you, that Jesus sent and gave to you.[16] You can see how they all work together. They're a team. They're your tribe.

John 17 speaks of how Jesus and Father God are one (unity) and in Each Other, and how you are one in Them. So, it should be clear that God (Father, Jesus, Holy Spirit) are in unity and union with Each Other, are with you, and are in union with you, always. And They certainly will be with you on your journey.

---

[13] John 16:7, AMP
[14] Matthew 28:19
[15] John 3:16
[16] Luke 24:49 AMP

The three most important members of your tribe are Father God, Jesus, and the Holy Spirit. I'm glad that I am in them, and they are in me. And they are one with you too! They are permanently in your tribe. And you are in Theirs. What a terrific start to realizing who is truly in your tribe!

ANGELS

I bet you didn't see that one coming! Did you know that you have an angel assigned to you at birth?[17] Did you know that angels are assigned to watch over you?[18] After experiencing the unfairness of a false accusation levied against you, that may not feel true, but it definitely is! Angels can also bring you revelation from God,[19] and can wage war against Satan and his demons.[20] Revelation from God, and having angels fighting Satan's demonic lies on your behalf, are definitely good resources to have while overcoming a false accusation. Angels can also give you direction on what to do or which direction to go, to help navigate you safely from harm.[21] And lastly, angels can bring you strength while you are weary and weak.[22] This is obviously not a complete inventory of what angels can do for you, but as you can see, partnering with angels can be very beneficial! Just simply thank the Holy Spirit for the help that angels can give and for their ability to do things that you cannot do, and ask the Holy Spirit to assign them to you to assist you moving forward on your journey of getting out of this mess.

OTHERS IN YOU YOUR TRIBE

We have already established that the triune God is leading your tribe, and that angels are available to assist. Ask God to show you

---

[17] Matthew 18:10
[18] Exodus 23:20
[19] Daniel 8:15-17 and Daniel 9:21-23
[20] Revelations 12:7
[21] Matthew 2:13 and Matthew 2:19-20
[22] Luke 22:43

who the other members of your tribe are—the people that God will give you to support you on your journey. Your tribe is simply your people. The people who will walk with you on your journey out of this mess. Your tribe won't judge you but will love, help, and encourage you. Your tribe will care about you. Your tribe will pray for you. Your tribe will stick with you. Your tribe will rejoice with you as God rescues you. Your tribe will treat you with dignity and honor. Your tribe will be there for you. Your tribe won't give up on you.

As you start to discover who your tribe is, some things may happen which might surprise you. Some people you thought you could count on may disappoint you. They may not be empathetic enough, care enough, or just don't understand why their support is such a big deal. I even had one person who knew I was innocent of these accusations take delight in watching me be miserable through the process. What made that betrayal even worse was that I had her back and came through for her on a couple of occasions—one was a raise in pay. If any of those things happen, ask God to help you not take up an offense. Immediately forgive and release them, even if you have to do it repeatedly. Let them go. Don't waste time and energy worrying about people who have opted out. They are not a part of your tribe for this journey. Move on. Keep working to find your tribe.

However, you may find people you did not anticipate who will be there for you. Be thankful for them. God has them with you for a reason.

MIGHTY MEN AND MIGHTY WOMEN

I always loved the story of David. There were so many things he had to face: lions and bears as a shepherd, a giant named Goliath who wanted to subjugate David and his countrymen under his thumb, his king who tried to kill him, and even a son who tried to kill him in a bid to grab the throne. David definitely faced treacherous times. But one aspect I love about David's story were his mighty men that stood by him. David's mighty men strongly supported him and were a part of his tribe. [23] And God will give you mighty men and women to strongly support you and to be by your side.

Most of your tribe who will strongly support you will obviously be your family and friends. Besides the Pastor I met on the train to the Grand Canyon, I was blessed with prayer warriors who strongly supported me. Once I opened up to the Pastor, he began to encourage me to find others. I received prophetic words as well. One prophetic word in particular described a gauge with the needle going full tilt one direction, and then suddenly full tilt the other—the interpretation was that the situation was going all against me, but God would intervene so that the situation would suddenly go all in my favor at the end. And that is what happened! That prophetic word was *very* encouraging! I could feel God's *peace* all over it! I needed people in my tribe who were willing to hear God on my behalf and speak to me what they heard. This is one way that Papa lets us know he's paying attention to our difficulty!

Another person had a prophetic word that my situation with the false accusation would be similar to Mordecai and Haman in the Book of Esther. In this story, the King of Persia took Esther to be his wife, which made her the Queen. Mordecai was Esther's guardian. Mordecai counseled Esther not to reveal that she was Jewish, as their family came from the conquered Jews exiled in Persia and could be viewed unfavorably. Mordecai discovered a plot to kill the King and informed the King of this plot. Because of that, Mordecai gained favor with the King.

---

[23] 1 Chronicles 11:10

Meanwhile, the King had an assistant named Haman. Mordecai would not show respect to Haman because of his dislike for the Jews. Haman became angry and wanted to kill Mordecai along with all the other Jews. Haman started building gallows for mass hangings of the Jews. But little did Haman know that Queen Esther was a Jew as well. Mordecai warned Esther of Haman's plans. Esther notified the King of this plot to kill her. The King had Haman killed on the very gallows originally meant for Mordecai and all the other Jews! That is basically what happened in my story. The dishonest manipulative conspiracy that was meant for my demise was discovered and caused my accuser's downfall instead. False accusations have been going on for thousands of years. Read the entire book of Esther. It's full of subterfuge, and you'll see how God takes care of people who are faithful to him.

ATTORNEY

Another member of your tribe should be an attorney for legal advice, counsel, representation, and protection. This is a decision only you can make for yourself, as you know your circumstances better than I. But unless the Holy Spirit is telling you an attorney will not be necessary, my advice is to get an attorney that has experience with defending against false accusations. Every situation is unique. Depending on your circumstances, they may advise you to fight, settle, or whatever, but they know the law.

YOU

Last, but not least, you are a member of your tribe as well. You are the one who has to live with yourself every minute of every day. So, don't forget to love yourself and take care of yourself. On this journey, you cannot help but get to know yourself better too. Although this is obviously not fun, but you will grow as a result of this. And what you gain cannot be taken from you!

ONE MORE THING . . .

One last parting scripture for your edification from today's sermon. Jesus who is in you is greater than the false accusation and accuser in the world.[24] There may be times where this doesn't seem true, but it is. You got this, because Jesus has got you! Now go forth, God in you and you in God! God will give you and your "mighty men" in your tribe the victory to defeat the lie! Amen!

Now let me turn it back over to the Pastor . . .

---

[24] 1 John 4:4

Chapter Five
Importance of Forgiveness

We sat down for breakfast early one morning. Marc filled his coffee and asked for eggs, one piece of toast with no butter.

I ordered the usual.

"No donuts today?" I asked. When Marc was in the middle of his case, as earlier noted, he gained a lot of weight. I'm afraid a lot of it might have been where we were meeting, as our usual place was called The Donut Hole, on Touhy Avenue. He always bought a dozen, and sometimes he'd eat three or four while we were talking, then take the rest of them to work with him.

"I'm working on my health, Pastor," Marc said.

"Good for you," I said.

"I'm still so angry," he said. "It just chews me up inside some days."

"Forgiveness is a process," I said. "When you have been falsely accused of a very serious accusation, it can be a very traumatic experience. But in order to heal and recover from the trauma, one of the most important steps you must take is to forgive your accuser. This may seem odd, repulsive, or impossible. You may feel your accuser does not deserve your forgiveness. You want justice for yourself, not leniency for your enemy. You want your accuser to repay you for the wrongs you suffered. You may even want to retaliate. This was personal. You want things to be made right for you. You want to be made whole.

"But, as much as you may desire all of these things, the path to freedom looks very different from you might have imagined it. The problem is that your accuser cannot pay you back for what they took. Forgiveness places you in a position where God can restore you and give you restitution. Here is how Jesus recommended we deal with those who mistreat us. 'For if you forgive others their trespasses—their reckless and willful sins—your Heavenly Father will also forgive you. But if you do not forgive others—nurturing your hurt and anger with the result that it interferes with your relationship with God—then your Father will not forgive your trespasses.[25] That is what Jesus said during His Sermon on the Mount. Forgiveness is important to God."

Marc looked at me and said, "Yes, Pastor. And if you are anything like me, you want all your sins forgiven by God, and not a one unforgiven. So I make it a high priority to make sure I forgive others. When I first read this many years ago, I thought forgiveness was to the benefit of the one who wronged me, as well as to make God happy with me. Back then, I thought forgiveness was like a merit badge of being a good Christian. But lately I have discovered that forgiveness is really for my benefit. I forgive because I enjoy God's free gift of forgiveness every day. If I am forgiven by God, who am I to not forgive others? God wants me to be free just like Him. God loves His enemies. He forgives us all. And God wants me

---

[25] Matthew 6:14-15, AMP

to treat others like He treats me. God wants me to forgive, as He has forgiven me, like Colossians 3:13 tells us. Forgiveness is for my freedom!

"It's not easy, though," he said.

"No, it's not," I said, thinking of all the times when I had been petty and unwilling to forgive when the wrongs done to me were so much more minor than what Marc has gone through. "But we all keep working at it."

MILLIMETERS VERSUS MILES

Marc and I kept reading scripture together. He read:

"Therefore the kingdom of heaven is like a king who wished to settle accounts with his slaves. When he began the accounting, one who owed him 10,000 talents was brought to him. But because he could not repay, his master ordered him to be sold, with his wife and his children and everything that he possessed, and payment to be made. So the slave fell on his knees and begged him, saying, 'Have patience with me and I will repay you everything.' And his master's heart was moved with compassion and he released him and forgave him [canceling] the debt. But that same slave went out and found one of his fellow slaves who owed him a hundred denarii; and he seized him and began choking him, saying, 'Pay what you owe!' So his fellow slave fell on his knees and begged him earnestly, 'Have patience with me and I will repay you.' But he was unwilling and he went and had him thrown in prison until he paid back the debt. When his fellow slaves saw what had happened, they were deeply grieved and they went and reported to their master [with clarity and in detail] everything that had taken place. Then his master called him and said to him, 'You wicked and contemptible slave, I forgave all that [great] debt of yours because you begged me. Should you not have had mercy on your fellow slave [who owed you little by comparison], as I had mercy on you?' And in wrath his master turned him over to the torturers (jailers) until he paid all that he owed. My heavenly Father will also do the same to [every one of] you, if each of you does not forgive his brother from your heart."[26]

"Look at this, Pastor," Marc said excitedly, "This is the parable Jesus told Peter, when he asked Jesus how many times he should forgive his brother. One slave's very large debt was forgiven by his master. I did some research on this. Based on values from June, 2018, a talent of gold would be worth about $1,400,000. Now multiply that by 10,000—which comes to 14 billion—14 billion dollars. Wow! The number is so large it is staggering! To put this in perspective, this slave was forgiven everything. That very same slave who was forgiven everything, did not forgive his peer who owed him far less. In that day, a hundred denarii equaled four months' wages. At minimum wage, that would be around twelve thousand dollars. If that wicked slave worked thirty years at minimum wage, it still would not even cover the cost of one talent, let alone ten thousand talents."

"Wow. You're right, those numbers are staggering," I said. "This slave lost perspective of what he had been forgiven. Jesus said in Luke 7:47 that one who has been forgiven much will love much. This slave did not love much at all, although he had just been forgiven of everything. God forgave us of *everything*. God expects us to forgive others for wronging us, even if it is a very serious false accusation that can ruin your life. From God's point of view, you are forgiving someone of something very little, compared to God forgiving you of not just something very big, but everything!

"Now look at this," I went on, "Earlier in verses 21-22 in Matthew 18, Peter wanted to know how many times he should

---

[26] Matthew 18:23-35, AMP

forgive someone. According to Jewish Law, Peter only had to forgive someone three times—that was the limit. Peter may have thought if he doubled the minimum and added one more, that would perhaps be generous. By Jesus answering 490—or, 70 times 7, Jesus was indicating that Peter needed to forgive without limit."

Marc grinned. "I for one am glad Jesus didn't put a limit on me letting him down and Him forgiving me. I am thankful I serve a gracious God who loves and forgives without limit!"

WWJD

Marc continued, "You know what I've thought about a lot? Jesus was falsely accused too. His false accusation led to his death by crucifixion. Crucifixion was the method of capital punishment used by the Romans by nailing the convicted to a wooden beam and left to publicly hang naked until eventual death by asphyxiation. What a brutal and humiliating way to die, right?!"

"That's true," I said. "And what's worse, the events before the crucifixion were also brutal. Jesus was betrayed by a friend. Jewish leaders plotted to arrest and kill Him. Jesus was continuously having to play the "gotcha game" with the Jewish leaders who were trying to prove blasphemy; they went all in on this plot at the end. He was mocked, ridiculed, and beaten while in custody before meeting with the Sanhedrin (the Jewish High Court), with the outcome already predetermined. They wanted him to be put to death; all the better if they could get the Roman government to do it for them. Jesus was also mercilessly whipped before getting crucified to the point He no longer looked human. A beating like that could tear off so much flesh you could be walking around with internal organs exposed. And despite all of that, Jesus still forgave them, during the last moments prior to His death. Luke 23:34 tells us he said, 'Father, forgive them; for they do not know what they are doing.' Wow! So you see, my friend, Jesus knows exactly what you are going through.

He has been there and done it! So let's follow His example and empowerment to forgive. It will bring freedom like you have never known."

"I gotta pray right now, Pastor," Marc said. To my surprise, he got out of his chair and dropped to his knees right there in the Donut Hole.

"Lord," he said, "I really took a beating but it's nothing like what you suffered for me. Please forgive me as I continue to work to forgive Melissa. I'm trying and still need your help with this. Sometimes I still feel bitter for the damage that she has caused, and it still really hurts. Thank you for your gift of forgiveness."

MERCY ME

Marc and I spent a lot of time discussing mercy. In the Beatitudes, Jesus tells us to be merciful (responsive, compassionate, tender), just as your (Heavenly) Father is merciful.[27] Judgement will be merciless to one who has shown no mercy; but (to the one who has shown mercy) mercy triumphs (victoriously) over judgment.[28] Showing mercy clearly has its benefits. God will show mercy to those who have shown mercy. God will be merciful when he judges you. It is the better way to show mercy to each other rather than to judge each other. This is consistent with how God treats us. We are to take on the character of God, which is mercy.

BE A FORGIVER AND NOT A FIGHTER

About a year later, I invited Marc to share his story with my congregation. He came on a Sunday and gave the message; I took notes on what he said. He shared a bit of his story about the false accusation, and then he broke it down for us:

---

[27] Luke 6:36, AMP
[28] James 2:13, AMP

"God is love and love does not take into account a wrong endured.[29] Because of your union with Jesus, you have His love, His heart, and His forgiveness inside you. So not only is it in your new nature to love, but it is also your nature to forgive.

"Never avenge yourself, but leave the way open for God's wrath and His judicial righteousness; for it is written in scripture, 'Vengeance is mine, I will repay, says the Lord.'[30] God wants you to leave the justice part to Him. Although it is tempting, do not retaliate. Forgiveness is trusting God's justice and you giving up your right to get even and settle the score. Doing so will ultimately feel hollow.

"See to it that no root of resentment springs up and causes trouble, and by it many be defiled.[31] Resentment can defile your heart. Your focus should be on forgiveness, so there can be peace and love in your heart so that you can move on. When you hold on to resentment, you are allowing those who have hurt you in the past to continue to hurt you today. Instead, let go of your need for them to make things fair or right with you. They can't. Leave that up to God.

"'Be kind and helpful to one another, tender-hearted, compassionate, understanding, forgiving one another, readily and freely, just as God in Christ also forgave you.'[32] God chose to forgive you. Forgiveness is a choice. Choose to forgive the one who has wronged you.

"Jesus told you to love and unselfishly seek the best, or higher good, for your enemies; make it a practice to do good to those who hate you; bless and show kindness to those who curse you; pray for

---

[29] 1 John 4:8 and 1 Corinthians 13:5, AMP
[30] Romans 12:19, AMP
[31] Hebrews 12:15, AMP
[32] Ephesians 4:32, AMP

those who mistreat you.[33] A big part of forgiving is to respond to evil with good. Pray that God will bless the person who willfully wronged you. This will ultimately set you free from them. Only the love of God inside you can enable you to do that. When someone falsely accuses you in hopes of ruining your life, only God's love can change your heart that God would bless them instead of wanting revenge.

"Included in your bulletin this morning is a sample prayer of forgiveness, along with a sample prayer for breaking a soul tie. When I was on my journey of freedom from my false accuser, I found it helpful to have someone walk me through prayers just like the ones below. I realized that I not only needed to forgive my accuser, but also realized that this traumatic experience touched my soul, and in essence tied my soul to my false accuser. I can assure you, I wanted no part of me to be tied to her, and vice versa. I hope you find these sample prayers helpful on your journey of forgiveness and freedom as I have. And it is okay to pray these prayers as often as is needed."

Marc had asked us to print these in advance and our congregation found them in the bulletin:

Prayer of Forgiveness:

Lord Jesus, by an act of my will, I chose to forgive <u>XYZ person</u>. <u>XYZ person</u>, I forgive you for <u>ABC thing(s)</u>. I release these things to you, Lord, along with the hurt and pain [you may name any other emotions such as anger, embarrassment, humiliation, confusion, guilt, shame, etc.] that they have caused. I release all of this to you, Lord, with the weight that has been carried in my heart and life, and I let it go. I ask you, Lord Jesus, to take back the ground in my life

---

[33] Luke 6:27-28, AMP

that the enemy had access to. Shut every door and lock every gate. Establish your Kingdom in this area of my life.

In the name of Jesus, Amen.

Prayer to Break Soul Tie:

In the name and through the blood of Jesus Christ, I break every tie to <u>XYZ person</u>. I separate my soul (my mind, my will, my emotions) from <u>XYZ person's</u> soul (his/her mind, his/her will, his/her emotions). I send back to <u>XYZ person</u> all of who he/she is, washed in the blood of Jesus. And I take back to me all of who I am, washed in the blood of Jesus. I ask you Lord Jesus to seal my soul and make me whole. Amen!

After Marc invited the congregation to pray one or both of these prayers aloud, he continued,

"You know, folks, scripture says that we will be known by our love; in this day and age, few things speak love to the broader culture than forgiveness. Hollywood has stories of revenge. When the news carries a story about forgiveness, people look at it and wonder. Check out the story of Andrew Collins and Jameel McGee, from Benton Harbor, Michigan. In 2005, Collins falsely accused McGee of dealing drugs, and McGee spent four years behind bars. You can bet that McGee wanted to hurt the guy who put him there! But Collins got caught and spent eighteen months behind bars himself for filing a false police report, planting drugs, and stealing. Later, both men found Christ. When they finally encountered one another again, McGee forgave Collins, and they began to work together toward racial reconciliation. That's really good news. That's the Gospel! If you've wronged someone, follow Collins' example and say you're sorry. And if you've been wronged, whether the other person asks for forgiveness or not, you've got to give it to them!"

I was glad to hear a variety of responses later from my congregation. One family told me that they had prayed to forgive someone who wronged them during the settlement of a grandparent's estate. They were working on repairing relationships with a couple of cousins. A husband asked his wife to forgive him for treating her with disrespect. Yet another person told me, "Pastor, that guy Marc preaches better than you do!"

"I know," I said. "I agree! I was inspired by his sermon. I'm even working on forgiving myself for all the boring sermons I've preached!"

Chapter Six
Renew Your Mind

And do not be conformed to this world [any longer with its superficial values and customs], but be transformed and progressively changed [as you mature spiritually] by the renewing of your mind [focusing on godly values and ethical attitudes], so that you may prove [for yourselves] what the will of God is, that which is good and acceptable and perfect [in His plan and purpose for you]. - Romans 12:2, AMP

Marc and I sat down early one morning as we debriefed the entire, traumatizing experience.

"It was really tough," I said, "to keep yourself mentally in a place where you could continue to function. You kept going to work every day. Some days getting distracted, to be sure, but you somehow managed. What was it?"

"You know, Pastor," he said, "When I first discovered the phrase "renew your mind" in scripture a very long time ago, I always thought it was a great idea. I figured not only would it be well with my soul if I continued to grow, but I figured it would come with the added benefit of knowing God's will for my life! That is *exactly* what I wanted and needed! That's the promise, right? But how? How does one renew their mind? I wanted to start right then, as I was in college, desperately trying to discover God's will on what I should major in. I thought at the time, if there was ever a time to know God's will, it would be now, while I was in the throes of deciding on what to do with the rest of my life. I was nineteen. I didn't realize it at the time, but I didn't know myself. And I surely didn't know God. There were a lot of people I looked up to and wanted to be like, so I would pick and choose the attributes I admired about them and try to become like them. But I wasn't being authentically myself, but an amalgamation of others."

"Sure," I said, "few of us really know our purpose at age nineteen; we have a constant process of renewing our mind, being transformed, and things become clear and even open up in different ways as we reach new levels of maturity. So, what did you do?"

"What I needed was a teacher to show me how to actually be myself, hear from God, and then to teach me how to do what God says, while being myself. I needed to learn how to renew my mind. I needed someone to teach me how to be myself with myself and be myself with God. I fortunately was blessed with a man about fifteen years older than me, who taught and discipled me. He was both patient and a good teacher. God blessed me with the discipleship I desperately needed."

"That's great, Marc," I said. "And I guess I've been able to help you this time around."

"Definitely, Pastor. I think with each new phase, we find new people to help us."

You may be wondering: what does renewing your mind have to do with a book on false accusations? Renewing your mind is actually a huge part of successfully overcoming any false accusation! Mind renewal is what overrides the false beliefs and lies that you have, or are currently believing about yourself, about God, and the situation you are facing. If we are going to win the battle against darkness and move forward in victory and wholeness, it makes a lot of sense to believe what God says about you, what God says about Himself, and what God says about overcoming the enemy, doesn't it? You, or the person you are walking beside, are going through a traumatic experience due to a false accusation. And through that, you may have unknowingly started to believe lies about yourself, God, Satan, and what your accuser is falsely saying about you. Renewing your mind is more than being mentally tough, so you don't break. It means leaning into God in the hard times to try to find the growth, like a grape vine during a drought reaches deeper in the dry soil for water, and this improves the quality of the fruit. What is the mindset? The mindset is of roots going deep in the face of disaster. Here are a few ideas we worked on as we thought about how important this topic is for someone going through a false accusation.

THOUGHTS HAVE TO OBEY JESUS

The weapons of our warfare are not physical [weapons of flesh and blood]. Our weapons are divinely powerful for the destruction of fortresses. We are destroying sophisticated arguments and every exalted and proud thing that sets itself up against the [true] knowledge of God, and we are taking every thought and purpose captive to the obedience of Christ. - 2 Corinthians 10:4-5, AMP

God has given you weapons to destroy lies that are contrary to what God says about you, as well as weapons to take every thought captive, whether they are your thoughts or thoughts from the enemy. For true mind renewal, the thoughts that enter your mind have to be obedient to what Jesus says about you. You have the power to arrest and stop untrue thoughts, rendering them powerless, as you kick them out of your mind. As you repeatedly do this and replay them with what God is saying, you won't even start to believe any lie or untrue idea that Satan wants you to believe about yourself. You have that power to destroy and expel lies out of your mind, so that you will not even start to believe a lie once you have identified it. Jesus helps you win again!

It may seem strange at first, but you can speak to your negative thoughts out loud. "Mister Mind, you must be obedient to what Jesus says about me."

You can also use your imagination. Imagine yourself as a kindly police officer pulling over those thoughts and arresting them, or a tough Western cowboy telling those thoughts "Jesus said there's not enough room in town for the both of us." Imagine watching those untrue thoughts turn and walk away, out of town, never to return.

YOUR MIND IS GUARDED BY PEACE

Do not be anxious or worried about anything, but in everything [every circumstance and situation] by prayer and petition with thanksgiving, continue to make your [specific] requests known to God. And the peace of God [that peace which reassures the heart, that peace] which transcends all understanding, [that peace which] stands guard over your hearts and your minds in Christ Jesus [is yours]. - Philippians 4:6-7, AMP

Jesus doesn't want you to be anxious or worried, even in the midst of enduring your false accusation. Continue making your requests to God, being thankful that God is handling your requests. This makes your focus on God and with being in communication and relationship with God. His supernatural peace will guard your heart and mind even under the worst accusations and on your worst days. Picture a big powerful angel called Peace that has spiritual weapons to constantly guard your mind. Any thought not from God is not allowed entry.

EXERCISE

Draw a picture of the Angel of Peace guarding the entry to your mind. Maybe that's your eyes, your ears, or your heart—it doesn't matter where. It also doesn't matter if you're not "artistic"—stick figures are okay with the Lord! Ask Jesus to show you little details to add to the Angel, and if you're worried that the drawing won't make sense, it's okay to label the details He shows you.

THINK ABOUT THE GOOD

Finally, believers, whatever is true, whatever is honorable and worthy of respect, whatever is right and confirmed by God's word, whatever is pure and wholesome, whatever is lovely and brings peace, whatever is admirable and of good repute; if there is any excellence, if there is anything worthy of praise, think continually on these things [center your mind on them, and implant them in your heart].- Philippians 4:8, AMP

Here is another great scripture that will help you maintain your peace, as you stand for the truth to come to light in your situation. It tells us to meditate on good things, not your false accusation and the possible ramifications from it. As you can see, there are plenty of good things to think about. Ask yourself these things as questions and journal your answer. If you're not sure, look up some of the suggestions and allow your mind to soak in the peace.

What's going on in the world or my life that is right and confirmed by God's word? (Find a news story about something like the Collins and McGee story mentioned earlier.)

What is pure and wholesome? (Just watch some puppies playing on YouTube!)

What is lovely and brings peace? (Perhaps finding a piece of artwork, dance, sculpture or photograph, or get out in nature for a walk.)

What is admirable and of good repute? (Find a person in your community who is doing good work, maybe the person who is in charge of your local food pantry or soup kitchen and admire and support their reputation for good in the neighborhood.)

What is excellent or worthy of praise? (Double down on the questions above and journal about it, thanking God for that excellent thing.)

There are lots of ways to actively meditate on this scripture!

YOU HAVE THE MIND OF GOD

Let's do a quick review of a basic principle of the New Covenant. The New Covenant is actually a covenant between Jesus and Papa.[34] Since both are in unity and in union with each other, and both are incapable of breaking a promise or a covenant, The New Covenant will last forever:

- Psalm 89:34 - God will not violate His covenant.

- Numbers 23:19 - God doesn't lie.

- Deuteronomy 7:9 - God is faithful and keeps His covenant.

- Hebrews 6:18 - Impossible for God to lie.

Think of a covenant like a marriage. Everything the husband has fully belongs to the wife, and reciprocally, everything the wife has fully belongs to the husband. In the New Covenant, everything Jesus

---

[34] John 17:10

has belongs to Papa, and everything Papa has belongs to Jesus.[35] Since we are in union with Jesus, everything Jesus has is yours as well, including His Mind! So, you have the same mind that Jesus has! Awesome!

Also found in scripture, it says that you have the mind of Christ (to be guided by His thoughts and purposes).[36] So, it is pretty clear that you already have the same mind as Jesus. In essence, your mind is already renewed. Isn't it great to know you have access to His perfect, flawless mind?! This is another truth for you to savor and meditate on during this process, as God rescues you from your false accusation.

You can ask, "Jesus, what are your true and renewing thoughts about me today?" or, "Jesus, speak to me about the purpose you have for me now, even if I don't completely understand it, I just want to hear your voice," and journal your answer. Don't worry at first if it is "right," but trust Jesus when he said, "My sheep know my voice,"[37] and you'll recognize him when he speaks. You can also talk to a mentor or pastor or any other mature Christian in your tribe and ask them to confirm the words you're hearing by saying together, "Does this sound like something Jesus would say to his disciples?"

If the answer your tribe comes up with is "yes," then you're hearing from Him!

SUPERNATURAL MIND RENEWAL (SMR)

Marc was especially adamant about SMR.

"One of the ministries that I wholeheartedly recommend, that played a big role in helping me hear from God and agree with what

---

35 John 17:10
36 1 Corinthians 2:16, AMP
37 John 10:27

He was speaking to me during the season that I was being falsely accused, is something called Supernatural Mind Renewal (SMR)."

"Huh, what is that?" I asked.

"SMR sessions are a great tool for renewing your mind. These sessions are guided by someone specially trained in SMR ministry; they help illuminate past events, overcome self-imposed limitations, and help you experience supernatural transformation. These sessions will help you connect with God. The Holy Spirit will uncover and transform your thoughts, emotions, and beliefs (both conscious and subconscious) that are driving negative behaviors, causing you pain, or are limiting you in some fashion. I have personal experience with SMR sessions, as I have completed over a hundred of them myself."

"That's a lot of sessions!" I said.

"Yes," Marc said. "As you can see, I take having a clear, renewed mind very seriously, as scripture says to be continually renewed in the spirit of your mind, having a fresh, untarnished mental and spiritual attitude—like Paul tells us in Ephesians 4:23 AMP.

"I have experienced miraculous breakthrough and freedom because of these sessions—they are based on Romans 12:2—are Holy Spirit-centered, and scientifically proven. I highly endorse anyone needing help with mind renewal to pursue this as an avenue for supernatural healing and transformation. This can be of great help!"

"Sounds amazing," I said, where can people get that?"

Marc gave me the links: https://www.inthesafeplace.com or https://catherinetoon.com; see these for more information and a way to book an appointment as you feel led. May you succeed and prosper and be in good health, just as your soul prospers.[38]

Marc definitely had a battle on his hands for many months. He used all of these scriptures to continue to work at renewing his mind. Some days were better than others—that's part of being human—but if you're right in the thick of things, focusing your mind on the positives in this chapter could be a lifesaver for you, so don't read this just once; make sure to come back to this chapter whenever you need a boost and do some of the exercises.

---

[38] 3 John 2, AMP

Jesus doesn't want you to be anxious or worried, even in the midst of enduring your false accusation.

Chapter Seven
Trusting God

"So you've been working on renewing your mind since age nineteen," I said. "With the help of a mentor. What else would you say was critically useful in getting you through the darkest days, the fear that you might end up in prison or on the sex offender registry?"

"You know, Pastor," he said, "A lot of the things that you can do to renew your mind, or to have a proper mindset, as a lot of people say these days, requires trusting God. You can hardly stop those negative thoughts and refocus on what is excellent, unless you decide that you'll trust God. Basically, worry and meditation are the same thing. If you worry, it means you are meditating on your problem and hoping you can solve it. But if you meditate on what is pure and true, you're hoping and trusting God to solve the problems that you're choosing not to focus on."

"That's interesting. So, worry is basically a negative form of praying to yourself?"

"That's a good way to put it," Marc said. "In my earlier years of walking with God, I found trusting God to be a hard thing to do. I trusted him more for others than myself. I trusted God some, but not all. I kinda trusted God, but I kinda didn't. Does God really have my back? I suppose that is why it takes faith to believe in an invisible God. But when you are going through a crisis, like a false accusation, trusting God may be all you have. When people are up against the wall or in the foxhole, they don't turn to their nice car, or nice house, or their good looks, or their ability to make friends, or their degree that says they are smart, or their own troubleshooting ability to save them. They turn to God, as the realization sets in that they need someone immensely more powerful than themselves and their own ability to rescue them. But take heart, trusting God is the best decision you could ever make. I have found the triune God (Jesus, Papa, Holy Spirit) to be the most trustworthy Persons I know and have ever met."

As Marc left behind the worst days and the false accusation became history, I invited him again to lead a workshop for our church on trusting God. The following sections are scriptures, encouragements, and exercises that Marc compiled.

JESUS IS TRUSTWORTHY

I have told you these things, so that in Me you may have [perfect] peace. In the world you have tribulation and distress and suffering, but be courageous [be confident, be undaunted, be filled with joy]; I have overcome the world. [My conquest is accomplished, My victory abiding.] - John 16:33, AMP

That scripture alone proves Jesus is trustworthy. After all, Jesus told us that we would have trouble and go through trials and distress and suffering. Obviously, enduring a false accusation and the ramifications it causes is definitely suffering and trouble. But Jesus told us to be courageous, as He has already overcome the world. And because of your union with Him, you too, have already overcome the world. Specifically in your case, you can overcome this false accusation that has turned your world upside down. Jesus conquering the world has already been accomplished. It is not something that needs to be done in the distant future that you would never see or experience. In fact, you are already victorious and have overcome the world because you recognize and believe that Jesus is the Son of God.[39] That faith of yours in Jesus is what entities you to that benefit. It is as simple as that.

FATHER KNOWS BEST

Trust in and rely confidently on the Lord with all your heart and do not rely on your own insight or understanding. In all your ways know and acknowledge and recognize Him, and He will make your paths straight and smooth [removing obstacles that block your way]. - Proverbs 3:5-6, AMP

For as the heavens are higher than the earth, so are My ways higher than your ways and My thoughts higher than your thoughts. - Isaiah 55:9, AMP

Sometimes, when you are in the midst of the battle for your life, it may seem like God doesn't know what He is doing, or how to help and protect you. You may even think or feel God is perhaps either away on vacay and not available at this time, or that He doesn't care, or that your situation may be tremendously lower on His priority list, or He may even be incompetent in this instance. None of this is true. God's ways and thoughts are better than yours. Don't try to step in and help Him out.

For example, it is silly for a child in kindergarten to help their parent write a business plan, while the parent continuously and patiently and lovingly says to not worry about it and that it is under control. It is foolish if that child persists in whipping out the crayons and tries to write and override what has already been brilliantly laid out on paper. In the same way, it is silly for you to try and

---

[39] 1 John 5:4-5

commandeer God's plan for you. The better way is to partner with God as your senior partner and follow His lead. God knows what will work out best for you. He already knows what lies ahead for you. Trust that God has the better plan, and the better way, for you. Jesus will clear the path for you, removing obstacles on the path, or even navigating a better detour to your victorious destination.

Here's an interesting exercise: Get a box of crayons. Again, your artistic ability has nothing to do with this, because you're imagining yourself as a five-year-old you. Draw a picture of God's Family Business Plan. Write down things that you are sure to be true. This might be a very short list, and that is the point, you don't have lots to add, otherwise it would be your list. If you can't think of anything else, you can start with:

"Jesus is trustworthy."

Then color the list, decorating it with a picture of you, Papa, Jesus and Holy Spirit. Feel free to add a house and tree and sun, keeping it simple. Maybe they run the family business out of a workshop in the back. Stick an angel in there if you want. It's your drawing.

JESUS WILL COMPLETE THE MISSION

I am convinced and confident of this very thing, that He who has begun a good work in you will [continue to] perfect and complete it until the day of Christ Jesus [the time of His return].
- Philippians 1:6, AMP.

This scripture tells us that we can be confident and convinced that Jesus will finish His good work in us. I think we all would consider Jesus rescuing you from a false accusation to be a part of this good work. In fact, Jesus will use it for your benefit. He will use it to grow your faith and trust in Him. He will use it to prove to you that He is trustworthy. He will use it to teach you how to be the overcomer that you are in Him. Through this current place of pain, Jesus will show you how to reign, graduating with a PhD from the Kingdom in this area. He will also empower you to help others on their way to overcoming their unique battle. Jesus will not abandon His work in you and leave you as incomplete. Jesus will not leave you hanging, never to return.

Another way to think of it would be to use the analogy from the famous movie franchise Mission Impossible. Satan always thinks he can outsmart God. Jesus always accepts the "impossible" mission of saving you and rescuing you while everything seems hopeless. Jesus likes playing the hero, because He is a hero, and He will be the champion you so desperately need. He considers His job to save, rescue, and protect you. Jesus is self-employed and loves what He does!

Exercise: Draw a picture, write a story, or make up a rhyme or little song with a common tune like Mary Had a Little Lamb, about Jesus as a superhero. Put yourself in it being rescued!

GOD'S PROMISES CAN COME FROM OBSCURE PLACES

When a man's ways please the Lord, He makes even his enemies to be at peace with him. - Proverbs 16:7, AMP

This is a powerful promise for those facing impossible odds. And the best part about this scripture is that you don't have to be perfect in and of yourself to please the Lord! Because of your union with Jesus, Father God is as pleased with you as He is with Jesus. Because of His great pleasure for you, He will make even your enemies be at peace with you. I found this scripture in particular to be of great comfort. It was a perfect scripture at the perfect time for me while I was enduring the investigative process.

Those who love Your law have great peace, and nothing causes them to stumble. - Psalms 119:165, NASB

Although in an obscure location in scripture, this was another timely and encouraging verse that gave me great comfort. Since I love Jesus and his law (or ways), I have great peace, and nothing causes me to stumble. It was amazing the peace I had while meditating on that scripture while enduring my false accusation. Despite great external turmoil, I had greater inner peace, knowing that Jesus would not let me stumble from a bold lie.

Both of these verses carried me. I could feel God all over them. I knew they were timely and unique for me. I could feel God promising me that I would be okay through those verses. I could feel God's peace and love and joy and faith inside me, assuring me whenever and however many times necessary, that I was going to be okay, that He was going to take care of me. I could also feel Satan's lies and fear coming near me, but immediately flee, like a magnet pushing another magnet away. All the circumstances and decision makers were aligned against me, all but One—the One that mattered.

Obscure-places exercise: Find an inconspicuous place in your house or drive around in your town looking for an obscure street, maybe a little closet or a dead end cul-de-sac with just a few houses—a place that doesn't seem important. Or think of an acquaintance in your life that Jesus might encourage you with, such as someone who was nice to you back in high school. Once you've chosen something obscure to focus your thoughts, ask Jesus to remind you of a scripture that you wouldn't normally think of, and to show you how he wants to encourage you from that obscure place.

This will help reassure you that Jesus is with you everywhere!

WHEN I LEARNED TO TRUST THE LORD

I have always been fascinated with stories about people listed in the Faith Chapter (Hebrews 11). They are listed because they trusted God. Abraham left his homeland by faith because he trusted God. Sarah had a child in her old age because she had faith to trust God. Moses delivered the Israelites from Egypt because he had faith to trust God. Moses also walked on dry land through the Red Sea, was led by a cloud by day and a fire by night, because he had faith. David had faith to trust God that he would be king, while the current king was trying to kill him. Joseph endured betrayal by just about everyone, but still had faith to trust God. Joseph ended up ruling and managing the greatest, most powerful country on Earth in his day. Noah had faith to trust God to build an ark due to the coming flood, even though he had never seen rain before.

I have been walking with the Lord for over 30 years, and I had my fair share of fantastic experiences. Yes, I am a dentist, but I have also been a pastor, a life group leader, been on prophetic teams and prayer teams, and have even been a team leader for a healing team. I have seen people healed. I have seen people give their life to the Lord and be born again. I have seen minds blown and lives changed by prophetic ministry. I consider all of those to be miracles, as those were great experiences to be a part of.

Some may be surprised that I would consider walking through the season of being falsely accused, which was like walking through the valley of the shadow of death, to be my best experience. But thankfully the Lord helped me walk through and encouraged me not to set up camp in that dark valley. He got me to the other side. It was like the beginning of A Tale of Two Cities: both the best of times and yet the worst of times. It was during that time of being persecuted with false allegations and harassed with serial investigations, when everything cratered around me and I could not help myself, that the Lord taught me to trust in Him. Learning to fully trust Jesus is priceless. Everything that has happened in my life and ministry since then has sprung out of that time when everything was imploding around me. That time brought such clarity to my life and purpose. It was during that time that the Lord really taught me to trust Him with my life.

It is not what comes out of you when everything is going well that determines the measure of your relationship with Jesus, but when everything falls apart that you find out the depths of your relationship with Him. What is your response to the Lord going to be? Will you trust Jesus? Will you let Him help you do so? Jesus is the only One after all who can save you.

Exercise: With a pen or pencil or those crayons, make a statement—even write it as a contract.

I hereby declare that I, _____________, will on this date _____________, trust Jesus with _____________________ until his work his complete.

Signed: _______________________________

Then choose a scripture from the previous chapters that speaks the most to you, particularly one where Jesus promises to be trustworthy.

Jesus hereby declares in book ______ verse _______ that he is trustworthy until the end of time. Signed: *Jesus*

Chapter Eight
Develop Your Faith

I sat down with Marc again. By this time, we had become friends. No longer was I supporting him as he walked through a difficult period; we were talking together as peers. He was doing more ministry, and it was an inspiring adventure for me to spend time with him. In spite of the difficulty of his situation, Marc asked the Lord to protect his mind and learned to trust, and I saw change in him: confidence, boldness. I wasn't sure exactly what to call it. Well, it's always best to get the news straight from the horse's mouth, as my grandfather used to say.

"What is the next step, after people have guarded their mind and begun to trust in Jesus? I get a sense that your faith has been growing," I said.

"Yes," he said, "I certainly hope so. I'd be so lost without it!"

"So, here's an interesting question," I said, "how would you explain the difference between *trust*, which we already talked about, and *faith*?"

"Well, you sure can't have faith without some measure of trust established. When you have been falsely accused, it can be terrifying! Day after day, you can feel the fear building. At times, it feels like it is impossible to muster any needed faith to believe God will rescue you. I know—I have been there. That feeling of hopelessness is suffocating! But fortunately, Jesus already has all the faith that you need. And after already reviewing the new covenant section in chapter 7, you already know that you have His faith! So take heart, it's not your job to fight this battle in your own strength. Jesus will fight this battle for you."

Marc started scribbling on a napkin and before I knew it, he had an outline for a talk on Faith.

"Boom," he said, "Here it is!" His notes turned into the meditations on scripture in the next section:

WHAT IS FAITH ANYWAY?

Now faith is the assurance (title deed, confirmation) of things hoped for (divinely guaranteed), and the evidence of things not seen [the conviction of their reality - faith comprehends as fact what cannot be experienced by the physical senses]. - Hebrews 11:1, AMP

One way I think of faith is: although I have not seen it happen yet, what I hope for is true and real. So, faith is the confirmation of something hoped for that is divinely guaranteed, and also factual evidence of what we cannot see, hear, taste, touch, or smell.

When I was going through my real-life nightmare, my continual hope and prayer was that the truth would come out clearly for all to see, along with the motives of the one making the false accusation in the first place. I had peace and assurance that my prayer was going to get answered in spades, and that I was going to be okay because the truth was going to come out during the investigative process, despite attempts to unfairly manipulate the outcome. And although it had not yet come to pass, it did not matter, because I knew deep down inside that it was true and that was all the evidence I needed to know the outcome was assured. That faith in God to protect me during those times brought me the peace I needed to see it through.

WHERE DOES FAITH COME FROM?

Let's go over a few more verses to help understand where faith comes from. Faith comes from Jesus.[40] Jesus is the *author* and *perfecter* of your *faith*.[41] Also, your faith is not only in Jesus, but also of Jesus.[42] So in summary, you already have the faith of Jesus as established by the new covenant and because of your union with Jesus. Jesus perfectly writes the faith needed on your heart and mind for your journey, and simply put, your faith comes from Jesus himself. Boom!

Every good thing given and every perfect gift is from above coming down from Papa.[43] We obviously consider faith a good thing, and as that verse says, faith also comes from Papa. So, not only do you have the same faith as Jesus, but the same faith as Papa! That faith that is given to you is pure and dependable, and is something you can count on!

WHY IS FAITH IMPORTANT?

Faith is very powerful. Jesus said faith the size of a mustard seed can move mountains, and that nothing will be impossible for you.[44] As you may remember from Biology classes, mustard seeds are very small, in fact, they are one of the smallest seeds in the Plant Kingdom. The faith that Jesus already placed in you is plenty, but even the smallest amount of that faith can achieve a great deal, even something miraculous. And I am here to tell you, friend, that I truly

---

[40] 2 Peter 1:1
[41] Hebrews 12:2
[42] Galatians 2:20, KJV
[43] James 1:17
[44] Matthew 17:20

consider the outcome of my investigation to truly be a miracle. The outcome was initially predetermined, and thanks to God, I came out clean.

Also in Matthew 13:31-32, Jesus said that faith can grow, from a tiny seed into a large fully grown tree of faith. The faith that Jesus gave you can grow into something very large.

You also please God by faith.[45] The faith that Jesus already placed in you pleases God, so you do not have to do anything to make God more pleased with you, because He already loves you and is pleased with the faith of Jesus and is in your corner! So you can see, the faith that Jesus gave you is powerful, can grow, and pleases God! Jesus helps you win again!

FAITH IN ACTION

What do you do when your situation seems to be getting worse? You put your faith in action by agreeing with God. Here are some exercises you can do to build that faith muscle—these can help you really live the promises scripture contains:

Exercise: Visualizing the victory and speaking faith-filled words will keep you in the faith zone (and not the discouragement zone or the fear zone) until the battle is won! Ask the Holy Spirit to help you use your imagination to envision your triumph over the lie. If you think it would help, write it out so you can read it , meditate on it, and declare it over your life.

So will My word be which goes out of My mouth; it will not return to Me void (useless, without result), without accomplishing what I desire, and without succeeding in the matter for which I sent it. – Isaiah 55:11, AMP

---

[45] Hebrews 11:6

Exercise: Speaking and praying the promises in scripture into your situation, along with declaring and decreeing your case to your situation, will energize you. It will bring confidence in your righteous standing and build your faith while you are on this journey to overcoming the false accusation. After all, when you pray and declare the word of God, it will accomplish and succeed in the matter for which it was sent. Praying scripture over your life is a game changer for those that want to learn how to pray and learn how to build your faith. I encourage you to apply that to any verse you find encouraging in this book.

Let's use two of my favorite scriptures as an example: Proverbs 16:7 and Psalms 119:165. And let's say a man named Joe was falsely accused by a woman named Sally. Joe can pray scripture into his life and situation like this:

Proverbs 16:7 (AMP):

When a man's ways please the Lord, He makes even his enemies to be at peace with him.

Now with inserting names, it would be: When *Joe's* ways please the Lord, He makes even *Sally* to be at peace with him.

Psalms 119:165 (NASB):

Those who love Your law have great peace, and nothing causes them to stumble.

Again, with inserting names, it could be phrased something like: *Joe* loves the Lord and His law (ways) and *Joe* has great peace, and nothing causes *Joe* to stumble, not even *Sally*.

A quick summary with bullet points:

- Faith comes from Jesus.

- Jesus perfects faith for you.

- You have the same faith that Jesus has.

- Faith is very powerful and can grow.

- Faith that Jesus gives you pleases God.

- You can exercise your faith to put into action, by meditating on and speaking out and writing down scripture.

Chapter Nine
Dethrone the Spirit of Fear

"I noticed that when you began talking about faith, Marc, you said that someone can feel the fear building day after day when they've been falsely accused."

"For sure, Pastor."

"So, you have guarded your mind, trusted in Jesus, invited him to build his faith in you, but you still have this fear going on, right?"

"Yeah, that's true."

"Fear has a function, doesn't it; to protect us? For example, you have a healthy fear of walking out into traffic, which protects you from getting hit by a truck?"

"Of course, but you don't walk around all day worrying about getting hit by a truck, either, do you? It would be paralyzing to have that kind of phobia."

"That makes sense," I said. "So, if fear is there even after you've gone through your mental protection, mind renewal, your trust and faith building, what do you do about it? What would you tell other people about how you've learned to deal with fear?"

"Good question," said Marc. "As I have mentioned before, when I first learned I was being falsely accused of sexual harassment, I was scared to death! My gut instincts immediately told me that this would be the fight of my life, as I did not underestimate what Melissa could accomplish. I figured if she was willing to tell such a big, bold lie about me, then she was willing to take this all the way. In particular, I was afraid of my accuser's ability to muster up so-called witnesses, as I had seen her manipulate many people into doing her bidding in an effort to have her befriend them, or at least not to be the object of her wrath and schemes against them. Looking back on it, it was both shocking and bizarre that adults, some who were professionals, would succumb to such foolishness. But then again, this wasn't just a natural battle. There were sinister forces of evil at work through my accuser. Not only was she an evil bully, but I believe the spirits of fear and intimidation were working through her. These spirits were what gave her such power to intimidate others.

"The Bible teaches us that the spirit of fear can be much more than just a strong emotion. And we're not talking about the kind of fear that makes you cautious to a normal degree, that prevents you from stepping in front of a speeding truck, either. The spirit of fear wants to pervert your faith, trying to convince you that, 'Papa's not capable enough or smart enough or powerful enough to take care of you, or that you don't deserve to have Papa take care of you, or that Papa does not love you enough to bother with taking care of you.' When we fear something that we have been deceived into believing is true (or have faith in), it is possible to enter into dangerous territory and start believing and agreeing with the lie that the spirit of fear is telling us, rather than what God says about us. It is appropriate to recognize the emotion of fear when there is danger present, as well as recognizing the lies that come from the spirit of fear; but we can walk in faith and definitely not fear. Perfect love casts out fear.[46] We can walk in faith because we are one with the Person of love, and faith works by love (Galatians 5:6).

"The spirit of fear is an evil spirit that can cause us to believe (have faith) that the very horrible thought that the evil spirit is intimidating you with is definitely going to happen, and that nothing can stop it. Agreeing with that spirit is what can make it so dangerous. As a believer, you are to believe and agree with what God says about you, along with what God's plans are for you, and definitely not what the spirit of fear is lying to you about you and your future. This spirit is attempting to paralyze you with fear so that you're inactive and ineffective!

"Whenever you are feeling anxious or fearful about your situation, the best thing you can do is to ask the Holy Spirit (your Helper) to reveal the lie that is driving that feeling. Then once you have identified the lie, ask the Holy Spirit to dethrone the spirit of fear by showing you the truth. This is what the Bible calls taking your thoughts captive.[47] And also in James 4:7 (AMP), we are to *resist the devil (stand firm against him) and he will flee from you.* So, by resisting to believe the lies from the devil and his spirits of fear, and also standing firm by believing the Truth the Holy Spirit speaks to you and your situation, scripture promises that the devil will flee from you, including his spirits of fear!

"All we have to do is believe the truth, and trust God to help you do so. That should be the extent of it. Agreeing and believing in what the spirit of fear is telling you is a torment that can snowball, and before you know it, you can start to believe there is no hope, that not even God can save you.

---

[46] 1 John 4:18, NASB1995
[47] 2 Corinthians 10:5

"Fear is the tool Satan uses to convince you that he is more powerful than God. It is what Satan uses to convince you that God is not strong enough, powerful enough, or smart enough to save you from this false accusation. Satan wants you to agree and believe what the spirit of fear is screaming at you will happen. Satan's goal is to discredit God, and in the process, ruin your life."

THIS IS WHAT THE LORD SAYS

"Hey, Marc," I said, "Let's see what God says about fear, along with anxiety and worry, which are just varieties of fear or ways of meditating upon the spirit of fear. Combatting fear must be important to God, as it is addressed frequently in scripture."

We began to dig, making notes together on our napkins, on the paper placemats, whatever we could get our hands on to write. The following are the highlights Marc compiled from that study:

God is love.[48] There is no fear in love, as love casts out fear.[49] As we have already established, Jesus is part of the Triune God (Papa, Jesus, Holy Spirit) living in you. Since Jesus is in you, His Love is in you as well. Since Love is in you, that means fear cannot coexist in you. In other words, fear wants to control you by dethroning love, but that is not possible as Jesus is sitting on the seat that controls the situation.

God has given you a spirit of power, love, sound judgment, and personal discipline (abilities that result in a calm, well-balanced mind and self-control). God did not give you a spirit of fear or timidity or cowardice.[50] I like how this scripture implies the difference between the spirit of fear versus the emotion of fear. And stating the obvious: that the spirit of fear did not come from God.

------

[48] 1 John 4:16
[49] 1 John 4:18
[50] 2 Timothy 1:7, AMP

What comes from God are His spirits of love, power, sound judgement, and personal discipline. All of these things give you qualities that result in you having a calm, well-balanced mind with self-control.

GOD GAVE ME HIS SPIRIT OF POWER

"It's not easy dealing with fear," I said to Marc. "It seems like it is always circling like a buzzard waiting for you to give up the ghost."

"Yeah. Don't give up on the Holy Ghost!" Marc said. "I remember when I was first accused of sexual harassment, fear was overwhelming me. I became timid. Fear temporarily made me a coward that did not want to fight back. I felt that fighting back might make things worse. What if Melissa decided to change her mind because she knew she was taking this too far? That was a naïve thought. Anyone who falsely accuses another, who is operating under the influence of a lying, accusing spirit, or what is referred to as a "Jezebel spirit," is not just going to back down and admit they are lying and want a take-back or a do-over. Spiritual battles must be fought with spiritual weapons. (We will touch more on the "Jezebel spirit" in the next chapter.)

"After about a month of hopelessness, I had an epiphany from the Holy Spirit! Truth would be my defense! From that moment on, I had a supernatural resolve to fight back and see this through. I told my supervisor that, "I didn't start any of this, but I'm going to finish it!" I stood up, looked her straight in the eye, and pointed at her while doing it, along with Rebecca and a Human Resource officer (the department that would manage the investigation) that were in the room. And I assure you, I made it clear that I meant every word of it. Not a single one of them ever heard me talk like that! Ever! And the thing of it was, that deep down, I could discern that all of them knew I was innocent too (well, Rebecca the union president obviously knew, but she wanted a certain outcome). My supervisor was more neutral than the rest, but the union and HR were married to a certain outcome, as bringing down a doctor would be an event that could enhance their careers and reputations, whether a promotion or a cash reward or a glowing evaluation, or perhaps all of those things. To my disappointment and shock, they were complicit in taking this whole thing too far, while my supervisor just got out of the way. But that did not deter them from moving forward with the outcome they were engineering. They chose the wrong side and pushed in all their chips.

"That supernatural courage and resolve was what God promised me in scripture. God has given me a spirit of love and power and a sound mind. That was a first for them, as they were not used to the risk-averse, rule-following, Boy- Scout doctor who avoided confrontation talking to them so powerfully, with such conviction, in that manner. From that moment on, the game changed because I changed. I was different going forward, and not the same nice guy, the guy who always grins and bears it, dutifully taking my beatings like I was their punching bag they had come to depend on. I think they fully expected me to lay down in the fetal position sucking my thumb, or die and let that buzzard, fear, get me, while they stomped on me until I was dead. God's power in me gave me the clarity of mind to boldly speak the truth. It was like Elijah against the 450 prophets of Ba'al and the 400 prophets of Asherah (1 Kings 18); me, against all of them. Because of that incident, I was labeled a troublemaker, someone who needed fixing, from that day forward. If having the audacity to defend myself from a false accusation of sexual harassment made me a troublemaker, then I was proud to be one! And just for clarification, I did not talk to them in anger or disrespectfully. I just boldly told them what was going to happen."

YOUR HERITAGE

"Yes!" I said, "Look, Marc! There are so many promises in scripture that declare your future victory. Triumph over your adversaries is your heritage in Christ. Through your union with Jesus, you, too, have overcome the world. One of my favorite passages of scripture that gave me strength during my own battles promises this: 'No weapon that is formed against you will succeed. Every tongue that rises against you in judgement, you will condemn. Triumph over your opposition is your heritage. That is your vindication from the Lord.'[51] Well, I consider fear to be one of the weapons that Satan uses against us the most when you are in battle. But scripture declares your victory. The spirit of fear will not succeed against you. Everything fear says in judgment about you, you have the authority to condemn. Defeating what fear says about you is your heritage. Your vindication from the spirit of fear is from God." Marc found some of these scriptures that point to victory and he shares them next.

YOUR ENEMY IS NOT A PERSON

Dear friend, one of the most important lessons to learn to keep in mind as you walk through the false accusation is this: your struggle is not against a person, but against the world forces of darkness, against the spiritual forces of wickedness.[52] Although it is very tempting to view your accuser as your enemy, your true enemy is Satan and his spiritual minions that mean you harm. Your accuser is merely their pawn. This is especially difficult to remember at times, especially when things get personal and ugly. But, it is also one of the most empowering. In the Kingdom of God, we are not given authority over people. We are given authority over the system of darkness. Through our union with Jesus and through the power of

---

[51] Isaiah 54:17
[52] Ephesians 6:12

the Holy Spirit, we can command Satan and his minions to cease and desist. By the name and through the blood of Jesus, we can speak to the storm of false accusations against us and command the truth to be revealed. Never underestimate your spiritual authority when you are facing a false accusation, even when it appears that your accuser has the upper hand. Stay strong and remember, the enemy is already a defeated foe. The only power he has against you is to convince you that he is more powerful than God Almighty. Don't fall for it and allow fear to rule your heart and mind during the crisis.

BE COURAGEOUS

Be strong and courageous, do not be afraid or tremble in dread before them, for it is the Lord your God who goes with you. He will not fail you or abandon you. - Deuteronomy 31:6, AMP

I love how empowering that scripture is! Be strong and courageous. Do not be afraid of your enemy. Do not tremble before your enemy. Since God is in you, God will not fail you. Always remind the enemy that if he messes with you, he will have to mess with God inside you! Satan wants to intimidate you and make you forget about your true identity. Turn the tables on Satan and remind him that you are the son or daughter of the King, and he doesn't want to mess with God inside you! Pummel him with that truth and constantly remind him that he is always a defeated foe!

Will fear always be there, lurking and circling like a buzzard? Yes, probably, at least in the short term. Fear is a major lie, and it is one of Satan's favorite tools. He's not going to stop using it any more than a burglar is going to stop trying to use his lock-picking tools to get into houses. But you've got a security system that's far more high-tech, and even if Satan stands outside all day wiggling and scratching at that lock with his favorite tool, the treasure God has placed inside you is protected. And remember: keep resisting what the spirit of fear is intimidating you with, and in doing so, that spirit of fear will flee from you. The more you resist, that circling lurking buzzard of fear will come around less.

LET JESUS TAKE CARE OF YOU

"Look at this, Pastor: This next scripture brought enormous peace to me on numerous occasions during my time of testing. 'Cast all your cares (all your anxieties, all your worries, and all your concerns, once and for all) on Him, for He cares about you (with deepest affection, and watches over you very carefully)'[53]. Isn't it comforting knowing that God actually wants to do everything for you, including taking care of you? But what is even more empowering is thinking about this scripture from a perspective of your union with Christ. Since you are in Jesus, and Jesus is in you, and Jesus has everything Papa has because They are one, you already have everything you need. Think about that for a moment. Jesus doesn't want you trying to fix your own problems, He wants to fix them for you. Jesus is waiting for you to 'refer' your problem to Him. Jesus is waiting for you to give Him permission to take care of you, your problems, and whatever else you are concerned about. And that definitely includes this false accusation you are dealing with. Jesus wants you to spend more time with Him—hanging out with Him, talking to Him, taking a walk in the park with Him, getting to know Him better, et cetera—and not time away from Him dealing with a problem that He can easily fix for you. Jesus will gladly take care of it, if you let Him."

DON'T WORRY, BE RIGHTEOUS

"But it's not just about being free from worry," I said, "or fear, for that matter. Jesus said do not worry or to be anxious about your life, because Papa knows what you need. But first and most

---

[53] 1 Peter 5:7, AMP

importantly, we are to seek His Kingdom and His righteousness, and all these things will be added to you.[54] You have His Kingdom and His righteousness already, as Jesus is in you. Your first priority, and the one that will bring the results you desire, should be with Jesus and spending time with Jesus first, and not worrying about your life. Jesus wants you to fulfill your Kingdom assignment while on this Earth, and not waste time worrying. Jesus and Papa already know what you need and want to take care of you. So spend time with Him as first priority, and everything else you are concerned about will be taken care of for you."

"Wow, that's really true," Marc said, "You know, even though the fear was lurking, and I knew I was a Boy-Scout type, I knew it wasn't my own righteousness that would save me. I had to seek His righteousness. And regarding His righteousness, did you know that the Holy Spirit convicts you of His righteousness?[55] Righteousness in the new covenant means more than right standing before God. Because of your union with Jesus, His nature inside you makes you righteous. It is an impartation. It is your true nature. Said another way, the Holy Spirit convinces you of His righteousness. It's like a constant and relentless reminder that you are righteous. Part of the lie that Satan brings is whispering that you are not worthy of His care, because you are not righteous. But even if you momentarily mess up, the Holy Spirit is there to immediately remind you that messing up is not in your nature, but your true permanent nature is righteousness in the Holy Spirit. Connecting with your righteous nature will help you believe that you are worthy as a son or daughter for Him to be strong on your behalf. This is another truth that I believe should empower anyone not to believe any lies said about you, but to believe what the Holy Spirit convicts and constantly

---

[54] Matthew 6:25-34
[55] John 16:8-11

convinces you of: that you are the righteousness of God in Christ Jesus.[56] You are as Jesus is in this world.[57]"

"That's great, Marc," I said. "And again, it puts your mind on a positive focus. It's not just running away from fear or worrying that fear will be a constant battle to overcome and resist, but running towards Jesus and His righteousness brings the positive focus."

Exercise: With some crayons, colored pencils, or markers, draw a locked door with Satan on one side, you on the other, and show what Jesus and His angels are doing—standing guard, protecting you or holding you—whatever comes to mind is okay. Add whatever details come to you. Then, ask Jesus what he wants to show you about his care for you in the picture and take notes on what you hear.

---

[56] 2 Corinthians 5:21
[57] 1 John 4:17

Connecting with your righteous nature will help you believe that you are worthy as a son or daughter for Him to be strong on your behalf.

Chapter Ten
Overcoming the
False Accusation

"Was it always like this at work?" I asked Marc one day.

"No, no, Pastor, it wasn't!" He replied. "Looking back, it is stunning to me how much chaos ensued shortly after Melissa was hired. Before her arrival, the dental offices were relatively drama-free and peaceful. People got along well with each other. People enjoyed being there. Communication was warmly professional and respectful. That all quickly changed when Melissa arrived on the scene. By her second week, there was already infighting and finger pointing. People seemed offended and betrayed by what others had said. Confusion and frustration quickly became the new normal due to her subterfuge. By the time the second month came, the office was in a state of disarray with no end in sight.

"As I said before, Melissa quickly befriended everyone. But behind the scenes, she was pitting people against one another. It was amazing how they would all run to her and confide in her for help and advice because they were upset, while she was the very one manipulating all of the situations that made them upset. She was causing the strife, but yet presenting herself as the one who would fix the problem she was causing! Alliances shifted every week or two. There was a dizzying carousel of frenemies. It was like all her followers were mesmerized by her, eager to do whatever she asked. It was as if they would do anything to stay in her good graces. They seemed blindly devoted to her."

"If everyone thought she was their friend, how did it all fall apart?" I asked.

"As time went on, cracks started to form. Her friendly requests became demands. Demands became threats. Her toxic tongue would publicly shame whoever was the object of her wrath. One of my co-workers was brave and started calling Melissa out, but Melissa quickly put her in her place and made an example of her for daring to question 'Queen Melissa'. What was once a 'friendship' became toxic intimidation for the one who had courage to stand up to her. Melissa's hostility in the workplace toward that brave soul was beyond egregious. It was like watching a bully in junior high terrorize their victim with impunity every day. It was disgusting!"

"How can this happen? Aren't they adults?"

Marc shook his head. "And due to protection from Rebecca, management was not taking complaints about her seriously. Melissa's 'enemy' finally left. She just couldn't take it anymore.

"As time went on, her 'friends' started doing what she wanted because they were scared of her, not because they wanted to be friends with her. It seemed like she could get anyone to do just about anything for her. It was surreal to watch adults, some who were highly-educated professionals, spy for her, lie for her, follow her 'orders,' and compete with others to stay in her trusted inner circle. It was as if she was the supervisor and everyone was gunning for a promotion, trying to out-jerk the others to be her trusted lieutenant. She ruled the roost. She had clean hands and her underlings doing her bidding were the ones with blood on theirs. It was a nightmare watching this unfold. A death by a thousand cuts, with the cuts being the days. I mourned the loss of what once was a peaceful place to work.

"Melissa didn't just upset the apple cart—she kicked it over and shattered it into pieces. She took the wood from that broken cart and beat people mercilessly into submission with it. For those that thought she was a bad leader, she wanted them dead! She let the apples spoil and become rotten. She made her followers eat them, convincing them that she was good by feeding them poison. It was beyond what you would consider normal work-place drama."

"It sounds worse to me than the T.V. show *The Office*," I said.

"Well, it sure wasn't that funny," Marc said. "In fact, it was supernaturally abnormal. It was evil. And in the process, I recognized that it was actually the work of an evil spirit commonly referred to as Jezebel."

"Yes, I've heard of that," I said, "so you're saying this was more than just a mean girl, it was a mean-girl-spirit."

"As I'm sure you can imagine based on the environment she had created, when Melissa lied and said I sexually harassed her, I was terrified of what she could accomplish, as she had proven skillful in manipulating people to do whatever she wanted them to do. Then when I realized Rebecca was in her corner with all the power of the union behind her, and marketing Melissa's story to management, it was then I knew I was in the fight of my life. I knew I was in way over my head. I knew it was me against the world. This battle was bigger than my ability to defend myself. I knew this was a spiritual battle that only God could rescue me from. And God did rescue me. And I will be forever grateful to God for that."

I realized that Marc was seeing another level of existence beyond the physical, material world. "What do you do when you're faced with this kind of attack? When it's not just something happening in the temporal realm?" I asked. I had some ideas, of course, but as a pastor I often ask questions and wait to see how people will answer. He shared the following insights.

WWJD

You shall not testify falsely [that is, lie, withhold, or manipulate the truth] against your neighbor (any person).
- Exodus 20:16, AMP

That is one of the Ten Commandments. It made God's Top 10 List. So, it must be pretty important to God. After my experience, I became more aware than ever that we, as believers, need to choose our words wisely about others—as loving neighbors we want to be careful with other people's reputations. Perhaps it starts with gossip. Little tidbits of drama feed the beast. It's as if you're feeding a python—it may not even need another meal for a while, it digests slowly—but the next thing you know, one day you wake up and you've got a twenty-five foot snake on your hands, and it's hungry!

Falsely accusing another person does not reveal God's character to the world, it reveals Satan's character. Satan is a liar who does what liars do. He lies, as that is what is natural for him. In fact, Jesus Himself called Satan the Father of Lies and half-truths. It is Jesus who always speaks the truth.[58] This may be stating the obvious, but it is imperative that we recognize the simple fact that lies come from Satan and the truth comes from Jesus. Furthermore, Jesus doesn't just speak the truth. He took it one step further when He said that He

---

[58] John 8:44-45, AMP

is the Truth.[59] So, not only does truth come from Jesus, Jesus is literally the Truth as well.

Satan accuses and brings charges against our Christian brothers and sisters before God day and night. In fact, Satan was thrown down out of Heaven by Jesus for accusing us.[60] If Satan is both a liar and an accuser, it stands to reason that this makes Satan The False Accuser. Satan is the one who is actually falsely accusing you. Unfortunately, Satan is also using a person to do the accusing. He is the one who is actually calling the shots and causing others to do his will.

In scripture, Jesus compares Satan to a thief who comes to steal, kill, and destroy, while describing Himself as the One who saves us. Jesus is the Good Shepherd who protects His sheep.[61] As your Good Shepherd, Jesus is also the One who is going to save you, protect you, and rescue you from Satan. Satan wants to steal from you, kill you, and destroy you, but thankfully, Jesus always looks out for us!

In summary, God does not like it one iota when someone is falsely accused. It is laid out in scripture very plainly. Satan lies because he is the Father of Lies. Jesus tells the truth because Jesus is The Truth. Satan is a false accuser because he is The False Accuser; it is his character and nature. Satan falsely accuses the righteous, judging them, telling them that they are bad and not worthy of God's righteousness. The Holy Spirit convicts you of His righteousness and constantly reminds you that your true identity and nature is His righteousness inside you. Satan wants to steal from you, kill you, and destroy you. Jesus wants to save you, rescue you, and protect you. The differences couldn't be more clear.

---

[59] John 14:6
[60] Revelation 12:10
[61] John 10:10-11

JEZEBEL

"I'd say the simple stuff is pretty clear to most people," I said to Marc, "so I think it would be helpful for people who are new to trusting Jesus to explain a bit more about who Jezebel is and why we call this kind of evil a 'Jezebel' spirit," I said.

"True," Marc said. "It comes from a fascinating story in the Bible about a false accusation involving Jezebel, a wicked queen of Israel in the Old Testament."

"Yeah, it's almost like a Disney movie, like one of Grimm's fairy tales, isn't it?"

"I mean, when you hear *wicked queen*, you can definitely use your Disney frame of reference to give yourself a picture, because she is painted the same way. So, she's married to Ahab, who was the King of Israel, which stands to reason, that's how you get to be the queen. So, Ahab coveted a vineyard owned by a man named Naboth. When Jezebel learned that Naboth was not willing to sell his vineyard to Ahab, she plotted to have Naboth killed. Pretty easy to grab his property if he's dead and you're the queen. She sent a letter to the leaders in Naboth's city with instructions. They were to arrange to have two men falsely accuse Naboth of cursing both the King and God, which in those times was a bad enough crime to have Naboth taken out of the city and stoned to death."

"And they followed the instructions to frame Naboth—because if they didn't, they were going to be next," I said.

"That's how it works. You do stuff to please the false accuser because you don't have the guts to stand up to her. If you do that, you put a target on your own back."

"Right," I said, "and it's on your back, not your front; they're going to literally stab you in the back, you'll never see it coming."

"Well. When word of the mission's success came to Jezebel, and this poor guy Naboth was dead, Ahab immediately took possession of Naboth's vineyard.[62]"

As you can see from this example, false accusations have the power to kill, ruin lives, destroy reputations, and to steal. And you can see how Queen Jezebel got a spirit of sinister plotting, framing, and false accusation named after her by modern Christians.

"Later in the story," Marc continued, "God sent the Prophet Elijah to confront Ahab about what he had done. Because Naboth was murdered to take possession of his property, God's judgement, under the covenant of the Law, was death to both Ahab and Jezebel. Ahab died in battle. Jezebel died after being thrown down, out of a window; her body was trampled by horses and ripped apart and eaten by dogs, which sounds about as horrible today as it was then. Satan rebelled against God, and was thrown down, and his girl Jezebel had the same fate. Her skull, feet, and the palms of her hands, were all that remained. Using typology, that symbolizes that her ability to think and talk, walk, and work remain. That could be a matter of semantics, but as Christians we should not empower spirits that Jesus has previously disempowered."

"Of note for clarification," I said, "There is no explicit reference in scripture for a 'Jezebel spirit.' This is a modern moniker for a certain type of evil. But I agree that those with discernment can spot a 'Jezebel spirit.' When they infiltrate a business, workplace, ministry, et cetera, all manner of disorder seems to ensue. We as Christians have authority over the enemy, which is Satan, and any willing accomplices who use Jezebel's methods of thinking and talking, walking, and laboring and working. Jesus in you is greater than that all day long."

---

[62] 1 Kings 21:1-16

"For sure," said Marc. "God looks at the Earth and sees everything.[63] Although Jezebel and Ahab thought they got away with having Naboth murdered so they could steal his vineyard, God saw it. He sent a prophet named Elijah to inform them of their judgement. Elijah predicted their deaths with gruesomely accurate detail; of course, when he did so, Jezebel threatened his life."

"What else would you expect her to do?" I said. Remember, the Ten Commandments forbid false accusations. A false accusation is one of God's top-ten most important prohibitions. God not only sees how you are being falsely accused, he will involve others to execute justice on your behalf. Romans 12:19 reminds us not to take vengeance into our own hands, but to leave it to God.

WINNING

*And they overcame and conquered him because of the blood of
the Lamb and because of the word of their testimony.
- Revelation 12:11, AMP*

You overcome Satan by the blood of Jesus, and the word of your testimony. As you already know, Jesus has already shed His blood for you. Your testimony is your story, your experience, your witness of events. Isn't it great that you can overcome Satan's false accusation against you with your testimony and the blood of Jesus that was already shed for you?! That's all it takes!

Scripture says to always be ready to give a logical defense to anyone who asks you. And see to it that your conscience is clear, so that every time you are slandered or falsely accused, those who attack or disparage your good behavior will be shamed.[64] So when asked, always have your testimony (your answer, your witness, your experience) ready to give, so that when you are falsely accused, your

---

[63] Job 28:24
[64] 1 Peter 3:15-16

accuser will be shamed. Of note, scripture said to be ready when asked, not seek out people to tell your story to when not asked.

GOSSIPING FOOLS

We've mentioned both false accusations and the tidbits of gossip that feed the baby snake. There are many verses in Proverbs addressing fools and gossip. I would definitely consider someone who goes around making bold false accusations against another to be both a fool and a gossip. You should not answer (or pretend to agree with) a closed-minded fool according to his folly. Otherwise you will be like him.[65] In other words, don't answer a fool in the same manner as the fool. Don't answer a fool who is angry and lies, with anger and lies yourself. Isn't that great advice?!

"Have you ever tried to reason with a 'crazy' person?" Marc asked me.

"We're not talking about mentally ill, are we?" I said.

"No, just a foolish person. I have tried on numerous occasions, and finally determined well into my forties that it is a waste of time. So basically, don't argue or try to reason with someone who is foolish, or with someone who is determined not to see your point of view. Common sense is borne out in the Bible. I think scripture is warning us to avoid being the target of retaliation and become unnecessarily ensnared and sucked into a fight, or argument, or even a false accusation. 'It is better for a man to meet a bear robbed of her cubs than the angry, narcissistic fool in his folly.'"[66]

"In other words," I said, "try to steer clear of, and avoid, someone you discern is angry, foolish, or narcissistic! As we already reviewed, sometimes a fool or a gossip or a false accuser cannot be avoided, as in your case. Perhaps Melissa could have been avoided

---

[65] Proverbs 26:4, AMP
[66] Proverbs 17:12, AMP

if you'd gotten out when your gut first told you to. Pay attention to your gut! But still be ready to tell the truth of your testimony —your experience of what you have seen—when asked, but do not seek a confrontation with a fool, especially one who is narcissistic, as their wrath could cause you harm."

"Right. Look at this verse," said Marc. "'A perverse man (or woman) spreads strife, and one who gossips separates friends,'[67] and 'For lack of wood the fire goes out, and where there is no whisperer who gossips, contention quiets down.'[68] So, gossip separates friends, and contention goes away when gossip goes away."

PRAY FOR YOUR ENEMIES

"We talked about vengeance," I said. "It's so popular in all the movies!"

"Right," Marc said, "This is what's known as the myth of redemptive violence. Instead of getting back at someone, Jesus said to pray for those who persecute you.[69] So, when you are mistreated or slandered or falsely accused or persecuted, Jesus wants you to pray for them! Although you may truly hate the person trying to ruin your life and career and reputation, and may even wish them a great deal of harm, Jesus wants you to pray for them, not against them. In fact, Jesus went so far as to say we are to love our enemies.[70]"

"That sure flips the idea of getting revenge on its head," I said. "It means instead of hating Melissa, you're required to care for her. How hard is that?"

"Right. Sometimes it felt near impossible," Marc said. "'Love is not provoked (nor overly sensitive and easily angered). Love does

---

[67] Proverbs 16:28
[68] Proverbs 26:20, AMP
[69] Matthew 5:44
[70] Matthew 5:44

not take into account a wrong endured. Love rejoices with the Truth. Love never fails.'[71] Since God is love, and you are in God and God in you, that means love is in you. His perfect love in you is what makes you have the capacity to actually forgive and love the person falsely accusing you."

"Certainly," I said. "So, since love never fails and does not keep score of wrongs you had to endure, that makes it tremendously easier to pray for your accuser, doesn't it?!"

"It makes it much easier," Marc said, "but I sure had my days when that was difficult teaching to put into action."

JESUS WAS FALSELY ACCUSED TOO

Jesus knows what you are going through. He was falsely accused too. Although he was questioned, no guilt was found in Him.[72] But the chief priests, Pharisees, ruling elites, etc., wanted to have him killed anyway. And as everyone knows, Jesus was crucified on the cross. Jesus let them crucify Him as He wanted to shed His blood for you and die for your sins. And because of His sacrifice for you, you are now in union with Jesus with access to all He has. And know that you can have fellowship with Jesus anytime, especially in the midst of your suffering.[73] And remember, Jesus wants you spending time with Him and not time wasted on fixing your problems—Jesus wants to fix your problems for you. So follow the better way and let Him help you by asking Him to help. Be encouraged. You are not alone. Jesus is standing by, ready . . .

---

[71] 1 Corinthians 13:4-8, AMP
[72] Luke 23:14
[73] Philippians 3:10

Jesus wants you spending time with Him and not time wasted on fixing your problems— Jesus wants to fix your problems for you.

CONCLUSION

I hope reading this book has been a blessing to you. My prayer is that the Holy Spirit spoke to you clearly while reading it. I believe the strategies and spiritual weapons Marc and I outlined in this book will prove useful for you if you will put them into practice. And remember, all of these principles are clearly outlined in scripture. They are not just for overcoming a false accusation, but they will help you overcome anything, really: abandonment or betrayal in your marriage; getting fired; getting sued for large amounts of money, or another life challenge. Pastors see these kinds of things all the time, and as we work with people, we see the Holy Spirit teach them through these scriptures in ways that are relevant to their situation and offer hope and salvation. The lessons you learn from your trial with a false accusation, or any other kind of trial, legal or spiritual, can be applied in any area of your life.

NOTHING NEW UNDER THE SUN

A man contacted my office and said he wanted to talk to someone, because he'd been falsely accused of sexual harassment. I thought to myself, well, here we go again. I called Marc.

"I got a call," I said, and, while keeping confidentiality, I sketched out the basics. "What's going on here?" I asked. "What's with this rash of false accusations in our culture?"

Marc sighed. "False accusations are not new to our generation," he said. "You're just more aware of them now. There are literally countless stories of others who have faced false accusations. There are stories in the news, my story, the guy who just called your office, stories from friends and family, and, of course, stories in the Bible."

"I suppose you're right," I said. In fact, scripture tells us "there is nothing new under the sun."[74] False accusations have been happening for millennia.

JOSEPH

This book would not be complete without mentioning how my all-time favorite story in the Bible is also a story that includes a false accusation. It is the story of Joseph.

If you're new to studying the Bible you might think this is referring to Joseph, Mary's husband. There's an earlier Joseph, a fellow who was a hero and a significant character in the ancient history of the Jewish people. If you've never read this before, you'll find the story of Joseph in the book of Genesis, beginning in Chapter 37 and continuing to the end of Genesis. If you're going through a false accusation right now, you need to read (or re-read) the entire thing!

Marc told me how encouraged he was to read this story again and again. "Look, Pastor. Did you ever notice that it was a false accusation of attempted rape from Potiphar's wife that landed Joseph in prison?"

"Of course," I said.

"And even though he knows God has promised him big things for his life, and he's really a leader in training, isn't it interesting how Joseph's original plan to leave prison was not successful? Joseph was hoping his ticket out of prison was from an acquitted cupbearer. In some ways that ended up being true, but not in the manner or timing Joseph was originally hoping for. Joseph's ticket out of prison came from God and His timing, when God afflicted

---

[74] Ecclesiastes 1:9

Pharaoh with the need for dream interpretation. I wonder if Joseph's attempt to leave prison as soon as possible, using his own ideas, delayed God getting him out of prison? But can you really blame him? Who wants to be in prison, let alone if you are innocent? What is the lesson here? God doesn't want you solving and fixing your own problems in your strength, using your intellect, in your timing. God wants to solve your problems for you. Yes, He wants to rescue you and save you, but all in His timing and in His way."

After walking together with Marc through his horrors, I realize it takes strength and patience and resolve to wait on the Lord. After the first few months, Marc began to guard his mind, refocus his trust and faith in Jesus, and believed he would be defended, but it's always tempting to jump ahead and try to get back to the good times. But God is faithful. He will deliver you in His timing. So let me offer you a word of wisdom and caution: God gave you a brain and expects you to use it. But, don't rely on your own understanding. Instead, spend time with God and rely on God. Seek Him, His Kingdom, and His righteousness first, and all the other things you need will be added to you.[75] Discern and follow His lead.

REMEMBER YOUR IDENTITY IN UNION WITH JESUS

I think the most important thing to remember from this book is what was outlined regarding the New Covenant. Remember that because of your union with Jesus, everything Jesus has is yours. That includes His wisdom, His understanding, His counsel, His strength, His knowledge, His love, His joy, His peace, His patience, His kindness, His goodness, His faith and faithfulness, His gentleness, His self-control, His mind. Everything Jesus has is already yours!

---

[75] Matthew 6:33

Remember, the New Covenant is actually a covenant between Jesus and Papa.[76] Since both are in unity and in union with each other, and both are incapable of breaking a promise or a covenant, The New Covenant will last forever:

- Psalm 89:34 - God will not violate His covenant.

- Numbers 23:19 - God doesn't lie.

- Deuteronomy 7:9 - God is faithful and keeps His covenant.

- Hebrews 6:18 - Impossible for God to lie.

It is important to remember and think of a covenant like a marriage. Everything the husband has fully belongs to the wife, and reciprocally, everything the wife has fully belongs to the husband. In the New Covenant, everything Jesus has belongs to Papa, and everything Papa has belongs to Jesus.[77] Since we are in union with Jesus, everything Jesus has is yours as well!

And most importantly, never forget: every good thing given and every perfect gift is from above coming down from Papa.[78] This means that God is holding nothing back from you. You are a joint-heir with Jesus. You are one with the King of Kings. The victory of Jesus is your victory. In Christ, you are more than an overcomer.[79]

HAPPY TRAILS

Marc's story has a happy ending.

After a couple of decades of dental exams, filling cavities, pulling wisdom teeth, and performing root canals, Marc realized that

---

[76] John 17:10
[77] John 17:10
[78] James 1:17
[79] Romans 8:37

his time as a dentist was drawing to a close. You can see that his passion for the Lord is infectious, and he loves to talk with people about the Lord. He especially focuses on working with people who are dealing with a false testimony, and he has a pastoral spirit about him. He now leads a ministry for people who are going through this kind of life-altering experience. He's positive, encouraging, and empathetic.

We worked on this book together, and I wanted to give Marc the last word:

If this book has helped you, I would *love* to hear your story and your testimony. I can sense the beginning of a ground swell forming that will cause a new movement. I can sense people starting to wake up to the unfairness and hypocrisy that can happen when people throw accusations around as if they are some kind of sick joke. Right now, people seem to get a kick out of humiliating someone else, when only fifty years ago, women who were truly raped, abused, and so forth, were ashamed to come forward. Society needed to hear those voices and has stepped up in many ways to protect women— no, it isn't perfect, but things have definitely improved. Now, we have made it safe for women who have been victimized to say so, and this has brought freedom. Along with freedom to speak out without shame, this freedom has left the door open for careless people to victimize others, accusing them shamelessly for their own personal or professional gain. We need new laws to protect people from the destruction that false accusations can cause: financial loss, job loss, reputation loss, and the deterioration of marriages under a type of stress only the strongest relationships can survive. I can see reformation of defamation laws coming. I can see God's justice and mercy and love, sweeping over America. Let's work toward a better future together.

Even if you are at your worst moment today, with accusations like a wrecking ball smashing your house down around you, know that you are not alone. Jesus is alive and inside you. So take courage and follow the Holy Spirit's leading. Seek help, too, from people. You'll need it! The work Jesus will do inside you will leave a lasting legacy here on this Earth. What starts with you changes the world!

ABOUT THE AUTHOR

Thor Stone loves helping men triumph against false accusations of sexual misconduct. As a survivor of such a traumatic experience himself, Thor feels called to provide godly hope, strategy, and a path forward for men to overcome the big lie and have a life of purpose. Thor is an author, consultant, coach, and speaker that helps transform men from bewildered victims to victorious overcomers.

For more information, see www.thorsstone.com.